HarperCollins*Publishers*
Westerhill Road, Bishopbriggs, Glasgow G64 2QT

www.collins.co.uk

First published 2004

Reprint 10 9 8 7 6 5 4 3 2 1 0

© Essential Works 2004

ISBN 0-00-7145047

Typeset by Davidson Pre-Press Graphics Ltd, Glasgow

Printed in Italy by Amadeus S.p.A.

CONTENTS

Checklists

INTRODUCTION

Saying 'Yes' is only the beginning. There are people to be told, arrangements to be made. A wedding is the public celebration of a private commitment for a couple. You want your wedding day to be special, to mark the beginning of your married life together, but where do you start?

While everyone agrees that getting married is one of the most stressful undertakings of your life, you should always remember that all of the preparations leading up to the wedding can be enjoyed too. The key is in the planning. If you have thought through all of the arrangements carefully, you will know that you have left nothing to chance and that certainly helps to reduce the stress factor and make all of the preliminaries a fun part of your whole wedding experience.

This book will help you to tackle what might at first seem like insurmountable problems and, although every wedding and every family is different, there will always be relatives and friends you can turn to for help or advice. Use *Gem Weddings* to decide how you want to approach your wedding and plan effectively for a wonderful, happy day.

1 THE ENGAGEMENT

Most couples have a period of engagement before their wedding, although the length of time is falling. It was the Romans who first introduced engagement rings, although the idea of engagements or betrothals is much older.

These days the proposal could as easily come from the woman, although statistics show it is still usually the man who asks the question. Traditionally, the proposal was made on bended knee, to suggest humility. It was also considered important that the setting should be memorable and romantic.

Engagements carry no legal obligations but they provide a useful period in which to reflect on the decision to marry. A certain amount of time is also needed to plan the wedding. On average, a traditional wedding will take about six months to organise, although a registry office ceremony could be arranged in weeks.

Asking permission

Most modern brides would expect to hear the proposal before a man asked permission from her father. However, it is not unusual for the man to speak to his fiancée's father shortly afterwards and this is a very good way to begin establishing a close relationship.

Family announcements

Couples today usually tell their parents together that they have decided to get married. It is traditional to tell the bride's parents first, but ideally both sets of parents should be told as soon as possible. This is best done face to face, but obviously if parents are on the opposite side of the world a telephone call might be the only option. At this early stage, it is important to make sure that there are no real objections to the marriage and that everyone is happy. Assuming that they are, they will want to spread the news – from friends and family, to Mrs Smith who used to smile at little Lucy when she was a toddler.

By tradition the groom should be congratulated on his engagement but the bride should be wished happiness.

ANNOUNCING THE ENGAGEMENT
✓ Do meet or telephone close friends and family to tell them the news.
✓ Do make sure close friends and family hear from you and not from each other.
✓ Do write to more distant relatives and friends.

✓ Do send the letters at the same time.
✓ Do keep a list of all those who should be informed of the engagement.
✗ Don't leave out anyone from either family. No one likes to feel excluded (even, and especially, great-aunts who haven't seen their great-niece or great-nephew since they were two).

Parents

If the two sets of parents have not met, it is a good idea to arrange for them to do so as soon as possible. If this is impossible, an exchange of letters or phone calls is an alternative.

Traditionally the parents of the future groom should contact the bride's parents to suggest a meeting. If lunch or dinner follows, it is the groom's parents who host the occasion and pay the bill.

Public announcements

Some couples may decide to announce their engagement in the national press, while others may prefer local newspapers as a good way to tell casual friends and acquaintances. It is customary for the bride's parents to pay for national press announcements, while those made in local papers are usually paid for by the groom or his family. However, many couples these days choose to write their own informal announcements.

NEWSPAPER ANNOUNCEMENTS

✓ Do send the announcement to the chosen newspaper at least a week in advance, clearly stating when you want it to appear.

✓ Do include a daytime contact number in case of any queries.

✓ Do make sure any handwriting is clear and all names are spelled correctly.

Here are some examples of notices of engagement for the press:

Mr S. Richards and Miss L. Spellman

The engagement is announced between Samuel Richards, elder son of Mr and Mrs David Richards of East Meon, Hampshire, and Lucy Spellman, youngest daughter of Mr and Mrs George Spellman of Ashbourne, Derbyshire.

Mr and Mrs George Spellman are pleased to announce the engagement of their daughter Lucy to Mr Samuel Richards, elder son of Mr and Mrs David Richards of East Meon, Hampshire.

Lucy Spellman and Samuel Richards

Lucy and Sam, together with their families, are pleased to announce their engagement.

Here are some variations.

If the bride's parents are divorced and the mother remarried:

Lucy, youngest daughter of Mr George Spellman of Ashbourne, Derbyshire, and Mrs Caroline Cox of Petersfield, Hampshire...

If the bride's father is dead:

Lucy, youngest daughter of the late Mr George Spellman and Mrs Caroline Spellman of Ashbourne, Derbyshire...

If the bride's father is dead and her mother remarried:

Lucy, youngest daughter of the late Mr George Spellman and Mrs Caroline Cox, stepdaughter of Jonathon Cox...

Obviously the same changes in wording would apply to the groom.

TIP: 'son/daughter of' usually means the only son or daughter.
'younger/elder' means there are two sons or daughters.
'youngest/eldest' means there are at least three brothers or sisters.

ENGAGEMENT RINGS

Engagement rings are a token of the promise that has been made to marry. They are not essential and some brides may prefer to save the money for something more practical. If you do decide to have a ring, it is important to remember that you will wear your engagement ring for a long time and it is worth taking time over your choice. It may be tempting to pick a very trendy design, but fashions change and it is often better to choose something more traditional or that suits your own particular style.

Some men like to surprise their new fiancée with a ring as soon as she has accepted their proposal, but more often couples prefer the fun of choosing together. It is conventional for the engagement ring to have been bought by the time the engagement is officially announced, but this may not be possible.

There are many options for where to buy the ring. Most couples go to a jeweller, but you may decide to commission your own unique ring from a jewellery designer or to buy an antique.

BUYING ENGAGEMENT RINGS

✔ Do choose a reputable jeweller or dealer.
✔ Do listen to recommendations.

✔ Do have any antique engagement ring you decide upon checked by a qualified assessor.
✘ Don't rush into your purchase.

Diamonds

The ancient Greek and Latin names for diamond mean 'unconquerable'. Diamonds were first used for engagement rings in the 15th century when Archduke Maximilian of Austria gave Mary of Burgundy, his bride-to-be, a diamond ring. They have remained the favourite choice ever since.

Diamonds are one of the hardest minerals on earth and are also used as abrasives and in cutting tools. The stones have been recognised and prized for more than 3,000 years but they must be cut to reveal their true beauty.

The value or quality of a diamond is judged on four elements, known as the four Cs: cut, clarity, colour and carat.

Cut is the most important of these elements as this is what makes the stone sparkle. Each flat surface cut into the gem is known as a facet, and the aim is for the facets to direct the maximum amount of light into the diamond and reflect it back, making the stone shine. Jewellers refer to the diamond's fire, which means the strength of the reflected rainbow colours, and the diamond's brilliance refers to the liveliness and sparkle of the stone.

Cut and shape are completely separate and not all diamonds can be cut into all shapes. This is why some stones of the same carat are more valuable than others. There are seven basic shapes for diamonds: marquise, round brilliant, emerald- or lozenge-shaped, oval-shaped brilliant, pear-shaped brilliant, heart-shaped brilliant and square. There is also a difference between old- and modern-cut brilliants, with modern-cuts being flatter.

Clarity Virtually all diamonds contain slight impurities or inclusions. These are traces of gases or minerals trapped within the stone which can look like feathers or minuscule crystals. Usually they can be seen clearly only by a jeweller using a special magnifying tool. The clarity of the diamond is the extent to which it is free from inclusions. Fewer than 1 per cent of all diamonds are flawless, which means they have no inclusions at all.

Colour Most diamonds are generally colourless, although they actually have a slight yellow or brown tone from trace elements in the stone. They are rated on a scale from D, meaning completely colourless, to Z. However, they can be quite definitely coloured blue, pink, red, green or yellow. Because of their rarity, these coloured diamonds are extremely valuable.

Carat The weight of the diamond is measured in carats and there are 100 points in a carat. Diamonds of 1 or more carats, the type used for solitaire rings, are now very rare and valuable.

TIP: *Don't be confused:* when applied to gold, carat means the amount of gold in relation to other metals in an alloy.

BUYING DIAMOND RINGS

✓ Do find a jeweller you are both happy with, preferably someone who specialises in gemstones.

✓ Do ask for a written valuation if you are spending a lot of money on a stone (you will need this for insurance).

✓ Do ask for an explanation if the jeweller uses terms you don't understand.

Setting

Diamonds are usually set in 18 carat gold or platinum. The style of setting is up to you. Popular styles include prong (or rivet), where the stone is held by small metal claws; cluster, where small stones surround a larger central diamond; bezel, in which a ring of metal holds the stone; bar setting, where each stone is held by vertical metal bars; and pavé (or invisible), where virtually no metal is visible between the stones.

Other Gemstones

Diamonds may be the most popular choice throughout the world, but there is no reason why engagement rings should not incorporate other gemstones. Emeralds, rubies, sapphires and birthstones for the month in which the bride was born are popular alternatives (see table on p.17).

Metals

When choosing an engagement ring you also need to consider the different metals available. Gold is still the most popular and most people opt for yellow. Red or rose gold and white gold are more expensive and often do not keep their brilliance as well as yellow. The amount of gold, or its purity, is measured in carats. The purest is 24 carat but this is too soft for most jewellery so other metal is added to make it more hard-wearing: 22, 18 and 9 carat golds are all suitable for rings. Platinum is even more durable. It is similar in appearance to white gold but much more expensive. Many gold Edwardian rings have a platinum setting for the gemstones because it is so hard-wearing.

TIPS: When choosing an engagement ring, remember:

- The ring should not be hard to slip on and should sit easily at the base of your finger.
- A toothpick should fit between the ring and your finger to allow for normal changes in size at different temperatures.

- Round-cut stones in a cluster are usually the most durable.
- The pointed ends of marquise and pear-shaped stones make them more vulnerable than other shapes.
- High, prong-set stones may catch on your clothes.

Hallmarks

The Hallmark Act of 1973 dictates that all gold wedding rings must be sold with a hallmark showing their quality. Engagement rings, which are often slimmer and more ornate, may be exempt.

Insurance

Rings should be insured against theft, damage, loss and, particularly in the case of engagement rings, loss of a stone. It is usually possible to add the ring to normal household contents insurance, but it should be listed as a separate item which is to be covered when worn away from the house. A jeweller's valuation of the ring may be needed by the insurers.

From the bride to her fiancé

It used to be the convention that the prospective bride gave her fiancé a gift in return for her own engagement ring and many modern brides still like to do this. In the past the engagement gift was often a signet ring or a tie clip. Other options might be cufflinks or a watch. Less traditionally, the present could relate to a particular interest or hobby. It is a token of the promise made and ideally should be something that will last.

Birthstones

Month	Stone	Meaning
January	Garnet	Truth and faithfulness
February	Amethyst	Sincerity
March	Aquamarine	Courage and hope
April	Diamond	Lasting love, joy and innocence
May	Emerald	Hope, happiness and success
June	Pearl	Purity
July	Ruby	Emotional contentment and love
August	Peridot	Understanding and inspiration
September	Sapphire	Repentance, emotional balance and wisdom
October	Opal	Lovableness and hope
November	Topaz	Faithfulness and joy
December	Turquoise	Domestic harmony and prosperity

TIME TO THINK

As soon as a couple become engaged there are plans to be made for the wedding. It is easy to be swept along by the preparations and forget that marriage is more than a wedding day. The most important thing a period of engagement gives a couple is time to think – about the commitment they are making and exactly what each wants from a marriage. Professor Larson, the head of Family and Marriage Therapy at Brigham Young University in Utah, believes most marriage problems can be traced to the pre-wedding relationship. In a book called *Shall We Stay Together* he has come up with a test for couples. The more they disagree with each other's views, the less successful they are likely to be as a married couple. Key areas where expectations may be radically different include children, work, finances, domestic chores and family.

The average age for first marriages is rising. It is now 27 for women and 29 for men. The fact that couples are older and more mature, and have often lived together before marriage should mean they are better prepared. But statistics don't always bear this out. Britain has the highest divorce rate in Western Europe, with one in three marriages doomed to failure. Today, one in eight children lives with a stepfamily. The National Stepfamily Association predicts that by the year 2010 most people will cohabit, marry, divorce and then remarry. Cohabiting is no longer frowned upon, there is no shame attached to having children outside marriage and with the abolition of the married couples' allowance there is no particular financial advantage to marriage.

And yet … a recent poll showed that three-quarters of the British population still believe in marriage and more than half feel it should be for ever. Year on year the number of weddings is increasing, and the weddings themselves are becoming more extravagant. More time, effort and expense are lavished on them than ever before. We have the growing cult of the celebrity wedding and, following the Marriage Act allowing secular weddings, couples can indulge their wildest fantasies, choosing locations as mundane as the local supermarket or as quirky as ice hotels.

The Archbishop of Canterbury has stated that living together is a private matter but marriage is a public affirmation of a couple's commitment to one another, and it seems that couples are still willing to make this commitment.

BREAKING OFF THE ENGAGEMENT

It is quite common to have doubts at some point during the wedding preparations and few couples never argue. But for some people, the closer they get to the wedding, the more they realise they are making a big mistake. It's never easy to admit you're wrong, but much better a broken engagement than to go ahead with the wedding knowing you're making a mistake.

Engagements are not legally binding and if you have decided to call off the wedding, it is best to contact family and friends as soon as possible with a minimum of fuss. If you can't face telling people in person, you can always write.

Cancellations should give only the names of the couple and the date when the wedding should have taken place. There is absolutely no need to mention any reasons why the engagement has been broken. If the engagement was announced in the press, it is usual to place a cancellation notice in the same newspaper:

> The marriage between Lindsay Clark and Mark Walker arranged for (date, time and place) will not now take place.

Any engagement presents should be returned to the sender and if wedding invitations have already been sent, a simple formal note should be posted to all guests:

> Lindsay Clark and Mark Walker regret to tell you that the wedding planned for (date, time and place) will not take place. Thank you for your kind wishes.

Or:

> Mr and Mrs Michael Clark announce that the wedding of their daughter, Lindsay, to Mr Mark Walker, arranged for (date, time, place) will not take place.

When the engagement is broken by the bride-to-be, etiquette suggests that she return her engagement ring. When it is the groom who has called off the wedding, his ex-fiancée may keep the ring, although she may prefer to hand it back.

RELATE:
Relate is a nationally registered charity with over 50 years' experience helping people with their relationships. It offers counselling, sexual therapy and other services to see couples through difficulties. It also runs marriage-preparation

courses called Couples which are open to anyone getting married, though people often attend at the suggestion of their vicar. The classes aim to improve communication and understanding and to avoid conflict.

Contact Relate on 01788 573241 or check out the website at **www.relate.org.uk** for further details.

2 WHAT TYPE OF WEDDING?

The first major decision is whether you want a religious or civil wedding. There are various legal criteria which must be fulfilled in order to be lawfully wed, but otherwise the type of service you choose, how formal or informal, traditional or quirky, is entirely up to you.

It is important to make this choice as a couple and that you are both happy with the final decision. Look at what is important to you both. Perhaps one of you is more religious than the other and feels strongly that they should be married in church. Parents may also have strongly held beliefs and it is up to you how far you take these into consideration, although if the bride's parents are paying a substantial part of the wedding costs, there needs to be some flexibility, and it is preferable that they approve of the arrangements.

There has recently been a resurgence in the popularity of big, elaborate weddings and the choice has never been wider. Couples are now free to marry in a country house or a castle, or even fly away to a tropical island if they wish. Yet increasing numbers are choosing traditional white weddings in church.

Whatever you decide, you must also be practical. Think about costs. Set a budget and stick to it (Chapter 6 will help you with this). You need to start thinking about how many people you want to invite to the wedding. Everyone involved will have their own ideas about who simply cannot be left out.

INITIAL PLANS

✔ Do talk to one another.

✔ Do discuss wedding arrangements with parents and close family.

✔ Do think carefully about what you really want.

✔ Do listen to others.

✘ Don't be pushed into something you are not happy with.

✘ Don't ignore parents' or close relatives' strongly held beliefs.

You will remember your wedding day for the rest of your life, so make sure it really is a day you are happy to remember.

RELIGIOUS WEDDINGS

Church of England weddings

The first step is to arrange a meeting with the minister of the church you have chosen for your wedding. He will be able to tell you if there are any problems with your choice and advise you of any specific procedures that are necessary (see Chapter 3, which outlines these).

Most couples choose to be married in a church with which they have a particular association. They may be on the church's electoral roll and worship there regularly, it may simply be the parish church for the area in which they live, or they may have a special long-standing connection with a church.

Neither bride nor groom has to be a Christian or to worship regularly in their parish church to be allowed to marry there legally. However, some ministers will only marry couples who have a religious commitment, and it is not unusual for vicars to discuss the emotional and spiritual significance of marriage. They may suggest a marriage preparation course or simply hold a series of relatively informal meetings to look at the ceremony and the vows being taken, and the issues involved in the bonds of marriage.

When first visiting the vicar, both partners should take along baptism and birth certificates. You will be asked to fill in a Banns of Marriage application form with details of birth and occupation, as well as those of your fathers.

It is important to arrange a mutually convenient wedding date and time with your minister as soon as possible. Many churches are booked a long time ahead, especially for Saturdays in spring and summer. Remember, with the exception of Jewish and Society of Friends' weddings, marriages in England and Wales are allowed only between 8 am and 6 pm.

Weddings have not been permitted during the hours of darkness since Hardwicke's 1753 Marriage Act. This was to put a stop to clandestine marriages and to women being dragged away against their will. At the time weddings did not have to take place in church and, in fact, most happened at home with a minister present to sanction the vows.

BANNS

Before a wedding can take place in church, the banns must be called. These are read aloud in church on three successive Sundays during the three months preceding your wedding and attest there is no objection to the marriage. If one of you lives in a different area, you must arrange for the banns to be read in the parish church there too and obtain a banns certificate to give to the minister marrying you. Your local minister will be able to advise you on exactly what needs to be done.

MARRIAGE SERVICE

The minister will ask which version of the marriage service you prefer.

Book of Common Prayer 1662 This is the oldest service and is usually thought rather archaic nowadays. The bride has to promise to obey her husband.

Book of Common Prayer 1928 This is an updated version with the same basic format but the bride does not have to promise obedience.

Alternative Service 1980 This has a more modern format and the bride can choose whether or not to promise to obey. It includes variations and a selection of prayers, psalms and hymns.

The new order of Common Worship This was published in November 2000. It has affected all church services, including marriage. There are new prayers and a variation on the wording of the vows and service. Your vicar will be able to explain the changes.

PHOTOGRAPHS AND FLOWERS

You should find out whether photographs, videos or other recordings are allowed inside the church during the ceremony. There may also be restrictions on the flowers you can have if you are marrying during a religious festival, so you will need to know about this before you order any. It may be worth checking whether any other couples are marrying on the same day in case you can share the cost of church flowers with them. Some churches will also arrange the flowers for you. More details on flowers, photographs and videos can be found in Chapters 10 and 11.

MUSIC AND BELLS

You should also ask about music. Some churches will allow only religious music, while others may be happy with a more secular choice. If you want to arrange your own organist you should speak to the resident organist first. Your chosen church may well have its own choir, but you should make sure they are strong enough to sing your preferred hymns or anthems. Most choirs and bell-ringers take a break during August and you should ask whether they are available. Churches often do not allow bell-ringing (even for weddings) during religious festivals such as Lent (Shrove Tuesday until Easter) and Advent (roughly the month leading up to Christmas).

Wedding music usually includes organ music before the ceremony, organ music or a hymn for the entrance of the bride, three hymns – one before the marriage vows; the second before the prayers, address and Bible readings; and the third after the blessing – a choir or organ piece during the signing of the register and music as the bride and groom leave the church. You may want a relative to read a lesson or a musician friend to play or sing during the ceremony. You should always speak to your minister about any special requests. There are specific details about the order of service, together with ideas for music and readings, in Chapters 17 and 18.

WEDDING REHEARSAL

The minister will arrange a rehearsal about a week before the wedding, so hopefully everyone will know what to do on the day and everything will go smoothly. Try to make sure that everyone is present. This is a good opportunity to make last-minute checks and adjustments to arrangements, and also for the best man and bridesmaids to get to know both sets of families. Some couples give their thank-you gifts to their attendants at the rehearsal, and the couple themselves may be handed presents.

Traditional wedding etiquette suggests that the rehearsal is a suitable time for couples to invite the minister to their reception. Often the invitation will be refused, unless the minister knows the couple or their families well.

CONFETTI

You should check whether your church allows confetti at weddings and tell your guests. Some churches object to the mess that is left behind from the coloured paper. Others may be quite happy for biodegradable rose petals or rice (that birds will eat) to be thrown.

COSTS

Certain charges are fixed by the Archbishop's Council of the Church of England, such as the publication of the banns and the basic church service. These are revised annually from 1 January. Other charges are variable and set by the individual parochial church councils – they can include fees for the organist and choir, for instance, bells, flowers, heating and lighting. Your minister will be able to outline these to you.

It is a good idea to pay the fees in advance, possibly at the rehearsal, rather than leaving them to the best man on the day. You may also feel it appropriate to make a special donation to the church, especially if the minister has been particularly helpful or made an extra effort on your behalf.

CHURCH WEDDING CHECKLIST

Fee

Church name .... ☐
Address .... ☐
Telephone no. .... ☐
Email .... ☐
Vicar .... ☐
Address .... ☐
Telephone no. .... ☐
Email .... ☐
Organist .... ☐
Address .... ☐
Telephone no. .... ☐
Email .... ☐
Choir master .... ☐
Address .... ☐
Telephone no. .... ☐
Email .... ☐
Bell-ringers .... ☐
Church available (dates and times)

....

....

Wedding date .... ☐

Dates for banns to be read 1... ☐

2... ☐

3... ☐

Dates for marriage preparation course	....	❑
Rehearsal date	....	❑
Additional fees due	....	❑
Total fees due	....	❑
Payment of fees		❑

Church of Scotland weddings

The main distinction of Scottish weddings is that they can be solemnised at any time of day and in any place. The bride's father might not give his daughter away; instead the minister may walk down the aisle to meet the bride and her father and then lead them to the altar. The father then takes his place next to his wife before the service begins.

For the Gaelic version of the wedding vows and Scottish wedding customs, check:
• **www.siliconglen.com**

Non-Church of England religious weddings

For religious weddings, other than those held under the auspices of the Church of England, to be legally valid in England and Wales, both the bride and groom must first contact their local superintendent registrar to make an appointment and apply for the appropriate certificate. If the wedding ceremony is to take place in a building not registered for marriages, there must be a civil ceremony first to make the marriage legal. It may also be necessary for a registrar to come to the wedding to register the marriage, if the officiating minister or priest is not authorised to register weddings. For further details, refer to Chapter 3.

Roman Catholic weddings

Catholic wedding services are similar to Church of England ceremonies. Arrange a meeting with your priest as early as possible and remember to take along both baptism and confirmation certificates. If both partners are Roman Catholic, the wedding ceremony is usually part of a Nuptial Mass and communion. However, there does not have to be a Mass and there probably won't be if only one of the couple is Roman Catholic. Remember, you need a dispensation if one of you is a non-Catholic and you should speak to a priest about this.

Other denominational church weddings

Methodist, United Reformed and Baptist church weddings are similar to Church of England ceremonies, although they are usually simpler. For specific details you should speak to the individual church minister. The preliminary preparations and basic format are broadly the same.

Remember to check whether your minister is authorised to register marriages.

CIVIL WEDDINGS

There are many different reasons why couples choose civil weddings. They may not share the same religious faith or may feel it is hypocritical to marry in a church whose beliefs have no significance for them. There may be family objections or they may be divorced and unable to remarry in a church. Some couples must also go through a civil wedding if they want their marriage to be legally valid, because their religious marriage ceremony is not recognised.

Whatever the reason, there are now more options open to couples choosing civil weddings than ever before. You can be married in any approved building and there are now over 2,000 venues in England and Wales alone which have been granted a licence by the local authority to hold civil weddings. The list includes stately homes, castles, hotels, museums, theatres, restaurants and even football clubs.

LICENSED WEDDING VENUES INFORMATION
For a complete list of licensed wedding venues, send a cheque or postal order for £5 made payable to The Office of National Statistics, to:

The Office of National Statistics
Local Services
Smedley Hydro
Trafalgar Road

Southport
Merseyside PR8 2HH
Tel: 0151 471 4200

Alternatively, you can telephone the Registrar General for England and Wales on: 0151 471 4817 for credit card payments.

For an online list of all the places which are now licensed to host weddings in England and Wales, check:

• **www.places-to-marry.co.uk**

Local libraries may also carry a copy of the list and your local registrar will be able to tell you of any licensed venues in your own area.

Wedding ceremonies in approved premises

Regulations still don't allow weddings to take place outside or in any sort of temporary structure, such as a marquee. Most forms of transport are also ruled out, although permanently moored ships may be a possibility.

When you have found your 'approved' wedding venue, it may not be very close to your home. Staff at the venue should be able to help you to arrange for a local registrar and superintendent registrar to attend your wedding and some even employ special wedding coordinators to help you plan your wedding.

As with all civil weddings, marriages in licenced premises should not contain any religious elements, although you can still include readings from poems, plays and novels.

CIVIL WEDDING VENUES

✓ Do ask friends for personal recommendations.

✓ Do visit the alternatives and look at them at the right time of day.

✓ Do consider what they will be like at the time of year you are planning to get married.

✓ Do remember to book registrars to officiate at your wedding.

✓ Do make an appointment with the registrar for the area in which you are to marry first. Only then contact your local registrar with all the details of when and where the ceremony is to take place. Both bride and groom must do this.

Register office weddings

Civil weddings at register offices are much shorter and less formal than religious ceremonies, lasting no longer than 20 minutes. If you are opting for a register office wedding, you should try to book the date and registrar when you first see the superintendent registrar.

Some offices are not always open and they may also be heavily booked at popular times of the year. Ask to see the rooms available for weddings – there may be several and you may have a definite preference as rooms are often specially decorated. You should also check how many people the wedding room can hold, since this will affect the number of guests you can invite to the wedding service.

There may well be several weddings taking place on the same day and it is important to arrive on time, ideally a few minutes early for your own ceremony (though not so early that you and your guests get mixed up with another wedding party!).

CIVIL WEDDING DOS AND DON'TS
- ✓ Do ask to see the marriage room(s).
- ✓ Do book in advance (but not usually more than three months).
- ✓ Do check whether you may include a reading in the ceremony.
- ✓ Do arrive on time for your ceremony.
- ✗ Don't arrive more than five minutes early.
- ✗ Don't arrive late.

MUSIC AT CIVIL WEDDINGS
Music should not be religious but it can certainly be included in civil ceremonies. Recorded music is

probably the best option for register offices, but live music may be possible at another licensed venue. Music may be played before the ceremony as the guests are gathering, for the entrance of the bride, during the signing of the register and again as the couple leave.

DRESS AT CIVIL WEDDINGS

There are no set conventions and couples may wear what they like. Usually this is smart but for the bride it can be long or short, a dress or suit, white or coloured; she may carry flowers or wear a hat or headdress. The groom normally wears a suit and floral buttonhole, but again it is entirely your choice. Do let guests know if you have a specific style in mind and a particular dress code.

SCOTLAND AND NORTHERN IRELAND

Civil weddings still have to take place in a register office. There are also residency requirements and you should check these in Chapter 3.

Alternative ceremonies

Vow-exchanging ceremonies reflecting your own beliefs and personalities are also possible. As these are not legally recognised, they can be held anywhere. If you want your marriage to be legally valid, you must also go through a civil ceremony. The British Humanist Association, tel: 020 7079 3580, will provide details.

Weddings abroad

For some couples, the idea of a romantic wedding abroad is irresistible. Not everyone is searching for a tropical paradise. Couples have been married at the top of the Empire State Building in Manhattan, on the giant ferris wheel in the Prater amusement park in Vienna and in tiny stone chapels on Tuscan hillsides.

Whatever your dream, there is probably a tour operator to help you. Many offer all-inclusive wedding packages that cover a church or civil ceremony, flowers, the wedding cake, a champagne reception, a wedding coordinator and all the paper-work, as well as a two-week holiday. They will advise you on legal requirements for marrying in different countries. If a wedding is legally binding in the country in which it takes place, it is probably legal in Britain too. Check with the tour operator, embassy or British high commission – and allow at least twelve weeks for all the paperwork to be processed.

When choosing a tour company, always use one that has been recommended, one that you have used before for holidays and that is a member of ABTA (Association of British Travel Agents).

TOUR OPERATOR WEDDING PACKAGES

The Travel Shop

• **www.travelshop.com** (excellent links and details of legal requirements for each country)

Abercrombie & Kent: 020 7730 9600

British Airways Holidays, or

• **www.batravelshops.com**

Couples: 020 8900 1913

Elegant Resorts

(Caribbean): 01244 897999

(European): 01244 897777

(Worldwide): 01244 897888

Elite Vacations' Island Weddings: 020 8423 3131

First Choice: 0161 742 2262

Hayes & Jarvis: 0870 898 9890, or

• **www.hayesandjarvis.co.uk**

Kuoni: 01306 747007, or

• **www.kuoni.co.uk**

Owners' Syndicate: 020 7801 9801

Sandals: 020 7581 9895, or

• **www.sandals.com**

SuperClubs:

• **www.superclubs.com**

Thomson: 020 7387 9321, or

• **www.thomsontravelgroup.com**

Tradewinds: 0870 751 0009

Travel à la Carte: 01635 863030

Tropical Places: 0870 160 5025, or

- **www.tropicalplaces.co.uk**
Unijet: 0870 5336336
Virgin Holidays: 0870 990 8825, or
- **www.virginholidays.co.uk**
Weddings and Honeymoons Abroad: 0161 969 1122
Also check the following websites:
- **www.get-married.co.uk** (stunning locations in Italy
for both religious and civil ceremonies)
- **www.hawaiian-wedding.com**

One of the advantages of marrying abroad is that
you can avoid months of preparation and it certainly
cuts down arguments about the guest list. However,
if you decide that you want your closest friends and
family with you on your wedding day, as long as you
choose somewhere not too far away, this is quite
possible now with so many tour companies offering
special deals for wedding guests.

You may also decide to have a second wedding
reception for relatives and friends when you return.
This way, they won't feel excluded and are still able
to join in your celebrations.

GETTING MARRIED ABROAD

✓ Do take originals of necessary documents, e.g. birth
certificates, decree absolute if divorced, previous
marriage certificate and death certificate if widowed.

✓ Do make sure you have a valid ten-year passport.

✓ Do take legal proof if your name has been changed by deed poll.

✓ Do take a legally valid declaration of parental consent if either of you is under 18 (or under 21 in some countries such as Sri Lanka and Kenya).

✓ Do check whether the country insists on any pre-wedding residency requirements.

✓ Do check whether the country has any other medical or legal stipulations – Mexico insists on pre-wedding blood and HIV tests.

✓ Do get a wedding certificate after the ceremony. Your marriage will not necessarily be registered in the UK. Contact the Office of National Statistics on 0151 471 4200 for details.

✓ If your ceremony is due to be held out of doors, do check on alternative arrangements if the weather is bad (it can happen).

✓ Do pack wedding dresses or suits separately or in special crush-proof boxes marked 'fragile' or check whether your airline can store them in the cabin for you.

✗ Don't forget to take out insurance.

✗ Don't forget to check what vaccinations you need.

✗ Don't forget sunscreen.

SECOND MARRIAGES

Most second marriages are civil ceremonies and they can be anything from a quiet wedding with only witnesses present to huge celebrations. Some religions have strict rules about remarriage and it may not be possible to have a religious ceremony. If you regularly attend a church you should speak to your minister. Each church has its own policy and it is entirely up to the individual incumbent. Your minister will be able to advise you about what is permitted and it may be that even if you cannot be married in a church, you can arrange a service of blessing to follow on from a civil wedding.

Couples often arrange second weddings themselves, which means they are freer from the constrictions of what parents and other relatives might prefer, but there may be other issues to consider, especially if you have children.

LEGALITIES

If you are marrying for the second time, you must have documentary evidence to show that your first marriage has ended. This should be either a death certificate or a decree absolute.

> **TIP:** *Always* make sure any documents are certified. The court which granted your divorce will be able to supply you with a certified copy. This will take about one week.

If you are marrying abroad, the decree absolute must be signed on the back by one of the district judges from the court.

FINANCES

This may be the last thing you want to think about, but joint finances are often more complicated to arrange second time around, especially if you own a house.

Consider talking to a financial adviser before the wedding. Make a will. Especially if you have children from your first marriage, you may want to ensure that any property or assets you own are passed directly to them.

CHILDREN

Children may be delighted about your wedding plans, but equally they may be feeling very uncertain about how they fit in and how they will be affected, especially if they are going to have to get along with new stepbrothers or stepsisters. Try to make sure they are happy about the marriage and reassure them if they were worried. Involve them as much as possible – perhaps they could be witnesses or have some special role in the celebrations.

There are no set rules about what works but plan carefully how you break the news. Do let their school know about the changing situation, and make sure a grandparent or favoured relative or adult friend is around to talk to your children to find out how they are really feeling.

SERVICE OF BLESSING

There are various reasons why a couple may not legally be married in church, usually connected with their differing religious beliefs or because one or both have been divorced, but it may still be possible to sanctify the marriage and confirm the wedding vows, made previously in a civil wedding ceremony, in church through a service of blessing. Services are at the discretion of the minister and you should contact your parish church.

Services of blessing are usually as much like a wedding ceremony as possible, but it will be made obvious that the couple are already husband and wife, so, for instance, the couple will walk into church together and the minister may say, 'This is the solemn vow that x and y *have* taken . . .', thus making it clear that this is a reaffirmation of vows. Since the couple are already married, the ceremony has no legal standing and the wording of the wedding service may be altered.

There is usually a short address, followed by readings and prayers to bless the marriage. It is possible to have a choir and hymns but you should speak to your vicar.

For more information, check:
• **www.cofe.org.uk**.

CHOOSING A WEDDING LOCATION CHECKLIST

How easy is it to get to? ❏

Look at access and parking – where will most guests be travelling from on the day? ❏

Size – is it big enough to accommodate all your guests comfortably? ❏

Can you hold your reception at the same venue? ❏

If not, is there a suitable reception venue nearby? ❏

Some venues will hold ceremonies only if the reception is held there too – check when you book. ❏

Make sure you know how long you are booking for. ❏

Are there hotels and guest houses nearby for you and your guests to stay overnight? ❏

3 THE LEGALITIES

Marriage is a legally binding agreement and couples are obliged by law to observe certain rules.

Basic legal requirements for marriage in the UK:

- Couples must give notice of their marriage.
- At least two competent adults must witness the wedding and sign the marriage register.
- The doors to the wedding must not be locked as the wedding ceremony must be public.
- The wedding must be conducted by a superintendent registrar or registrar in the case of civil weddings, an ordained minister of the Church of England or a legally authorised minister from another religious denomination.
- One partner must have been born male and the other female.
- Both bride and groom must be marrying by their own consent.

Who you may marry

Or who you can't marry. All close family members or blood relatives are considered too closely related to marry by law. When it comes to stepbrothers and stepsisters (or even stepfathers and mothers) the law is more complex. In some instances marriage is allowed, but only if the couple are over 21 and have not lived in the same household as each other while under the age of 18. First cousins may marry but it is wise to talk to your GP and check your family medical history.

Some in-laws are also excluded. For instance, a former father-in-law may not marry his son's ex-wife unless the son and the father-in-law's former wife have died. Both parties must also be over 21. Adopted children cannot marry their adopted parents, but they are allowed to marry other members of their adoptive family, even brothers and sisters. If you are in any doubt, you should contact your church minister or area superintendent registrar.

WOMEN MAY NOT MARRY:
Father
Adoptive father
Son
Adopted son
Grandfather
Father's brother or half-brother
Mother's brother or half-brother
Sister's or half-sister's son
Brother's or half-brother's son
Grandson

MEN MAY NOT MARRY:

Mother

Adoptive mother

Daughter

Adopted daughter

Grandmother

Mother's sister or half-sister

Father's sister or half-sister

Sister's or half-sister's daughter

Brother's or half-brother's daughter

Granddaughter

The age you can marry

Both partners must be over the age of 16. If you are under 18 (and have not been married before) you will need a parent or guardian's legal consent. If you don't have your parents' consent and you are being unreasonably refused, it is possible to appeal to a magistrates' court, the county court or the high court. If you wish to be married within the Church of England you will need parental approval.

Marriage in Scotland and Northern Ireland is legal from the age of 16 and as a last resort it is still possible to elope to Gretna Green, but you would first need to inform the district registrar of your plans to marry. (More information about Gretna Green is given in the section 'Marrying in Scotland'.)

Where you can marry

The 1994 Marriage Act changed the law for weddings in two main ways: local authorities can license 'suitable premises' for the solemnisation of vows, which means civil weddings no longer have to take place in register offices; and neither bride nor groom has to live in the district where they are being married. If you want to know whether it is possible to marry in a particular place, check with the local register office for that area or the General Register Office. Register offices cannot be booked more than three months in advance.

Religious weddings may take place in any church, synagogue or temple (with some variations according to specific religion) but, other than with the Church of England, you must also both make appointments with your local superintendent registrar.

You can find specific information on marriage, remarriage, mixed religious or interdenominational weddings and divorce from the various authorities.

- General Register Office: 0151 471 4803
- Local register office for nearby venues
- Libraries will also hold lists, and you can check:
- **www.places-to-marry.co.uk**

Essential documents

For any type of ceremony, both partners need certain documents.

- A birth certificate if either partner is under 23 years of age.
- In the case of second marriages you will need proof of the end of the first marriage. This can be a decree absolute or death certificate, but no uncertified documents are acceptable.
- Names and addresses.
- Fathers' names and occupations (this may not be applicable).
- If any of the documents are not in English, you will also need a certified translation by an approved translator. It is important to remember that it is a criminal offence to give false information.

Giving notice of your wedding

Every marriage must be announced or licensed before the wedding can legally take place. For Church of England weddings the announcement is made through the publication of the banns of marriage. For civil weddings and non-Church of England religious weddings, you must contact your superintendent registrar, who will make an entry in the marriage notice book.

Church of England and Church of Wales weddings

Weddings held in the Church of England are legal as well as religious ceremonies and there are legal requirements that have to be met before you can be married in a particular church.

Basically, if either you or your partner lives within the parish boundaries of a church, or is a regular worshipper and on the electoral roll of a church (that is, you have been worshipping there regularly for six months), you may ask to be married there provided there are no ecclesiastical bars. It is not ordinarily possible for a wedding to take place in church if either of you has been divorced, but you should always speak to your vicar.

If the church you have chosen for your wedding is outside the parish in which you live and you are not on its electoral roll, you must apply to the Archbishop of Canterbury for a special licence, but you will need a very good reason to support your appeal and will have to show a long-standing connection with the church.

BANNS

This is the cheapest and most popular method of making a marriage announcement. The banns are read out in the church in which the wedding is to take place on three successive Sundays prior to the ceremony, and state the names of the couple intending to marry, the parishes in which they live and the wedding date.

If either of you lives in a different parish from the one in which you are marrying, the banns must also be read in that parish church and you must have a banns certificate confirming that this has happened. The wedding must take place within three months of the banns being published.

The tradition of publishing the banns of marriage was introduced by the Archbishop of Canterbury in the 14th century. Anyone who knows of a just cause or impediment to the marriage is invited to come forward. It is usual for couples to come to church at least once to listen to their banns being read but at one time this was considered unlucky.

COMMON LICENCE

This is much quicker than waiting for banns to be read. You have to wait only one clear day before the licence is granted but there must be a valid reason for marrying quickly. To obtain a common licence, you must apply to the Court of Faculties in London or to your local bishop or his surrogate, and at least one of you must appear in person to sign a legal declaration that there is no reason why the wedding cannot take place, and that either you or your partner have lived in that parish for at least 15 days. Your own minister will be able to advise you.

SPECIAL LICENCE

A special licence has to be approved by the

Archbishop of Canterbury and is issued by the Court of Faculties. You would apply for a special licence to marry in another parish or in a building not approved for weddings. They are usually granted only in exceptional circumstances and you will need a very good reason, such as wanting to marry in the parish church in which one of you was baptised and worshipped regularly until only recently moving away. Even the royal family needs a special licence to marry in St Paul's Cathedral.

For more information on licences, contact:

• Court of Faculties, 1 The Sanctuary, Westminster, London SW1P 3JT. Tel: 020 7222 5381

CHURCH OF ENGLAND WEDDING CHECKLIST

Vicar's telephone number ....

Meeting with your vicar (date)

Take along: birth certificates ☐

death certificate/decree absolute
(if second marriage) ☐

Banns organised ☐

Organise wedding licence/certificate if necessary ☐

Book wedding ☐

Other religious weddings

For all religious weddings other than in the Church of England, the legal requirements are the same as for civil weddings. Usually, you will also need to apply to the minister or religious authority for your own place of worship. If you want to be married in another area you will often need to prove you worship regularly or give notice in that area.

RELIGIOUS WEDDINGS

Church of England Enquiry Centre: 020 7898 1000, or
• **www.cofe.org.uk**
Church of Scotland Department of Practice and Procedure: 0131 225 5722
Marriage Care (formerly Catholic Marriage Advisory Council): 020 7371 1341
Methodist Church Press Office: 020 7486 5502
United Reformed Church: 020 7916 2020
Baptist Union: 01235 517700
Religious Society of Friends (Quakers): 020 7663 1000
Greek Orthodox Church Information Centre: 020 7723 4787
Office of the Chief Rabbi: 020 8343 6314
Jewish Marriage Council: 020 8203 6311
Muslim Information Centre: 020 7272 5170
The Hindu Society: 020 8944 0251

Civil weddings in England and Wales

The first step is to make an appointment to see the superintendent registrar of the registration district in which you live. You can find the telephone number and address in the telephone book under Registration of Births, Marriages and Deaths, and the law requires you to have lived in the district for seven days prior to giving notice.

SUPERINTENDENT REGISTRAR'S CERTIFICATES

The Marriage Act of 1949 was amended on 1 January 2001 and one of the main changes is that two superintendent registrar's certificates are now required for a marriage to be solemnised, even when both partners live in the same registration district. This means you must each go, in person, to your own local office and separate fees will be payable for each notice. Couples must wait 15 clear days before the certificates are issued.

At your appointment, an official will complete a form with both your names, addresses and ages. An entry will be made in the marriage notice book stating when and where you will marry. Couples usually book their ceremony at this meeting and, if you are planning to marry in a different area, you should book your date and time with the registrar of the district in which you want the wedding to take place before seeing your own local superintendent registrar.

ABOLITION OF CERTIFICATE AND LICENCE

The other major change to the marriage law from 1 January 2001 was the abolition of the certificate and licence which enabled couples to marry one clear day after legal notice had been given.

REGISTRAR'S GENERAL LICENCE

This allows a marriage to take place anywhere and at any time. It was introduced in 1970 and is really reserved for cases of serious illness, although it may be used in certain other special circumstances. This licence is valid for twelve months.

CIVIL WEDDINGS

Local superintendent registrar: for address and telephone number, look in the telephone directory under Registration of Births, Marriages and Deaths.

General Register Office for England and Wales:
0151 471 4803

General Register Office for Scotland: 0131 334 4447/4475

General Register Office for Northern Ireland: 028 9025 2000

Superintendent Registrar for Jersey: 01534 502335

General Register Office for Guernsey: 01481 725277

General Register Office for the Isle of Man: 01624 687039

British Humanist Association: 020 7079 3580

CIVIL WEDDING CHECKLIST

Appointment with superintendent registrar: ☐

bride (date) ....

groom (date) ....

Take along: birth certificates ☐

death certificates/decree absolute
(if second marriage) ☐

Fee for entry into marriage notice book ☐

Details of wedding entered in marriage notice book ☐

Organise marriage certificate ☐

Date for collection of certificate ....

Book registrar for wedding ☐

Look at ceremony room in register office ☐

Roman Catholic weddings

The legal requirements are basically the same as for
a civil wedding but you must obviously also apply to
your priest. The formalities take some time and it is a
good idea to do this as soon as possible, at least six
months before the wedding. You should also take
your baptism and confirmation certificates with you.

If both bride and groom are Catholic, banns will be
published. If one is not, you will need a dispensation
from the bishop to allow you to marry in a Catholic
church. It is best to speak to your own priest about
this. For the wedding itself, usually a priest is
authorised to register the marriage. If not, a registrar
must attend. For more information, contact Marriage
Care, tel: 020 7371 1341.

Jewish weddings

Again you must make two applications – one civil and one religious. The legal requirements are the same as for civil weddings. You should also apply to the religious authority for the area in which you are to marry and you will need to show documents proving you are Jewish.

Jewish weddings are exempt from the law stating all weddings should happen between 8 am and 6 pm, but Jewish law forbids them on a Friday or Saturday. The ceremony is usually held in a synagogue but could equally be performed in a private house or outside. They are solemnised under a canopy known as a *chuppah*.

Marrying in Scotland

Gretna Green was traditionally associated with eloping couples because it was one of the first stops across the Scottish border and it was possible to marry in Scotland by simply stating your vows in front of two witnesses. Scottish marriage laws have since been tightened but they are still slightly different from English rules.

The legal age for marriage in Scotland is 16 and parental consent is not necessary. Both bride and groom must give a marriage notice to the registrar of the district in which they are to be married.

The registrar then provides a marriage schedule. This takes at least 15 days but it is wise to hand in your notice around four weeks before you want to marry, and allow longer if it is a second marriage. The registrar brings the marriage schedule along to a civil wedding and afterwards the bride and groom sign and the registrar registers the wedding.

For religious weddings, the legal requirements are the same. Banns are not necessary but either the bride or groom should collect the marriage schedule from the registrar seven days before the marriage and give it to the minister or authorised person conducting the wedding. After the ceremony it should be signed and returned to the registrar within three days. As long as the minister agrees, a Church of Scotland wedding can take place anywhere, even outside.

If the wedding is to take place in England or Wales and only one partner lives in Scotland, they should apply for a certificate of no impediment or a certificate showing the banns have been read in the Church of Scotland. If you have any doubts or queries you should contact the registrar general at the General Register Office for Scotland, tel: 0131 334 4447/4475.

Marrying in Northern Ireland
CIVIL MARRIAGES

Just as in England and Wales, notice must be given to
the registrar of marriages for your district. The length
of time you need to have been resident in your area
depends upon whether you marry by licence or
certificate.

REGISTRAR'S LICENCE

This is issued seven days after the couple have given
notice. If both partners live in the same district, one
must have lived there for at least 15 days and the
other for at least seven. If both partners live in
different districts, they must each give notice to their
local registrar and must have been resident for at
least 15 days; the registrar for the district in which
the wedding is to take place will need a certificate
from the registrar of the other district before the
licence can be issued. The licence means that the
wedding can take place in any authorised premises
within that district. (This is not valid for Jewish or
Society of Friends' weddings.)

REGISTRAR'S CERTIFICATE

Both bride and groom must have lived in their
district for seven days. If they live in different districts,
notice must be given to the registrar for each. The
certificate, or certificates, will be issued 21 days after
notice has been given and copies must be sent to
whoever is conducting the wedding.

CHURCH OF IRELAND WEDDINGS

There are four ways to proceed if one or both partners are members of the Church of Ireland or other Episcopal or Protestant Churches:

1 Licence – if at least one partner has lived in a district for seven days, you can apply to the licensing minister for that district.

2 Special Licence – allows couples to marry outside their own parishes but there must be a valid reason for doing so. This can be granted only by a bishop and there is a set fee.

3 Registrar's Certificate – as outlined above. For this to be recognised in the Church of Ireland, either the bride or the groom must have lived in their church parish for at least 14 days.

4 Banns – both partners must be members of the Church of Ireland or another Protestant Church. As in the Church of England, banns are read out, or published on three Sundays in both the bride's and the groom's churches.

ROMAN CATHOLIC WEDDINGS

There are two ways to proceed for Roman Catholics:

1 Licence – issued by a licensor appointed by a bishop. If only one partner is Roman Catholic, the licence takes longer to arrive.

2 Registrar's Certificate – as outlined above. The certificate allows a wedding to take place in a Roman Catholic church within the registration district.

RELIGIOUS WEDDING (NOT C OF E) CHECKLIST

Minister's telephone number ....

Meeting with minister (date) ....

Take along: birth certificates ☐

    death certificates/decree absolute
    (if second marriage) ☐

Banns to be read (if applicable) ☐

Book wedding ☐

(plus all the steps for organising a civil wedding) ☐

MARRYING ABROAD

Marrying abroad is increasingly popular with couples. It is important to check with the embassy or high commission that your wedding plans are in line with local laws and are valid in Britain. You should also check for any specific requirements for the country in which you are planning to marry. The US, for instance, stipulates that couples have a blood test.

Always make sure you have a record of your marriage having taken place. If you are concerned, you can register your marriage with the British consulate which means it will automatically be registered with the registrar general in Britain. You could also register your marriage certificate or a certified copy with the Family Records Centre at the Office of National Statistics when you return. It is obviously much easier to obtain a copy from there than from a tropical island should you ever need one.

- The Office of National Statistics, General Register Office, Overseas Section, Smedley Hydro, Trafalgar Road, Southport, Merseyside PR8 2HH. Tel: 0151 471 4200

Or ask for further information from:

- The Foreign and Commonwealth Office, The Nationality Treaty and Claims Department,

Clive House, Petty France, London SW1H 9HD.
Tel: 020 7270 1500

If one partner lives overseas

The foreign partner must fulfil residency
requirements. If couples have already married in
another country, husbands or wives of British citizens
legally living in Britain must apply to join their
partner. You will have to prove that you can support
yourselves and any children and that your marriage
is genuine. For more information contact the
Immigration and Nationality Department.

- Immigration and Nationality Department, Lunar
  House, 40 Wellesley Road, Croydon, Surrey CR9 2BY.
  Tel: 0870 606 7766

CHANGING NAMES

There is no legal obligation for women to change their surname to that of their husband. Indeed, many women today choose to keep their surname, especially those who have built a successful career and feel that to change their name would be damaging. Some choose to keep their old, unmarried name only for work and this is perfectly possible, provided you tell relevant organisations such as your bank, employer and pension fund that you are known by both names.

UK law allows a person to use any name they choose – as long as it is either their birth name, the name adopted on marriage or a name changed by deed poll. It is less usual for a man to opt for his wife's name, but there is no legal reason to stop him and he may simply prefer his wife's. Some couples choose to use both surnames and create a double-barrelled one.

CHANGING YOUR SURNAME
✔ Do discuss the various options as a couple well before the wedding.
✘ Don't listen to other people's criticisms once you have reached a decision.

If you do decide to change (and this applies to men too), your name must be amended on official documents and there are various people and organisations who should be notified.

SAMPLE LETTER

Address you are   Your address
writing to   and telephone
                      number

Date

Dear Sir/Madam

Bank account no./Reference no./National Insurance no.

I wish to inform you that I will be changing my name from (old surname) to (new surname) following my marriage on (date).

Please let me know if you need any other information or documents.

Yours faithfully

CHANGING YOUR SURNAME CHECKLIST

Important documents to be changed:

Passport ❑

Bank account ❑

Credit cards ❑

Mortgage ❑

Driving licence ❑

Insurance company (car and house) ❑

Life assurance ❑

Pension fund ❑

People to notify:

Employer ❑

Doctor ❑

Dentist ❑

Tax office ❑

Local authority (Council tax) ❑

Library ❑

Sports clubs or other leisure facilities ❑

Changing your passport

If you have decided to change your name and want your passport to be in your married name, apply as soon as possible to the passport office. Don't leave it until the last minute. You can still travel under your old name until your passport runs out, but it is a good idea to take your marriage certificate with you to avoid confusion.

4 SETTING THE DATE

The next step after deciding where you are getting married is to set the date. This will be largely dependent upon the sort of wedding you have chosen. An elaborate traditional wedding will take longer to arrange than a wedding at a register office.

Many couples have a fixed idea of the season they would prefer, but you should also consider your guests. It is obviously better to avoid times when a lot of people will be away on holiday and while you may love the idea of a snowy midwinter wedding you should also consider how easy it will be for guests to travel.

For large or formal weddings you should realistically allow at least three months for planning. The shortest possible time to arrange an elaborate wedding is about six weeks (with lots of hard work and effort).

Churches, florists, caterers and photographers in particular all tend to be busiest during the summer and the most idyllic reception venues may be booked more than a year in advance. This is also the peak time for holidays, affecting your choice and the cost of your honeymoon.

Over 100,000 couples marry between the months of July and September. This doesn't mean that it is impossible to marry during the summer, it just means you should allow longer for arrangements. Be organised and book early.

TIME-CONSUMING ARRANGEMENTS	
Wedding venue	Flowers
Reception	Transport
Clothes	Photographs
Catering	

You know your own preferences, but also talk to the key people involved and find out if any times are difficult for them. The bride's parents may be paying for most of the wedding and be very involved in the plans, but don't forget the groom's family. Most weddings take place on Saturdays; a weekday or even a Sunday might give you a greater choice of dates but may be more tricky for guests.

Significant dates

There may be certain dates which have a special significance for you as a couple. Perhaps you share the same birthday or maybe you became engaged on the anniversary of your first meeting. You might enjoy remembering this date as your wedding anniversary each year.

Checking availability

When you have a rough idea of when you would like your wedding to be, find out exactly on which dates the ceremony venue is available. For church weddings this will depend upon how popular the church is for weddings and what other events are already planned. Register offices and other approved wedding venues may be just as heavily booked. If you have somewhere special in mind for the reception, you should also check the dates when it is available.

Choosing a time

When you check available dates with your ceremony and reception venues, you may find that only certain times are possible, in which case you will have to pick the one that suits you best.

Otherwise, decide what time of day you would prefer.

Some couples can't bear the thought of waiting around for too long on the day before the ceremony; others would prefer to have a leisurely time getting ready. You should consider any travel plans you have – for instance, if you are flying away on honeymoon immediately after the ceremony, and how far away you are staying for your first night together. If you are marrying in winter, remember it will be getting dark from mid-afternoon. Will most guests be travelling to the wedding on the day? How long are their journeys? Try to allow them enough time to arrive comfortably.

SETTING THE DATE CHECKLIST

Make a list of possible and impossible dates for all the key people involved in your wedding. ☐

Check what dates and times are available if you want a particular church or other venue for your wedding ceremony. ☐

If you have a favoured venue for the reception, check dates and times when it is available. ☐

Check dates for major national or sporting events. These should be avoided. ☐

Check the average weather – some months are surprisingly dry and others notably wet or windy. ☐

Booking

When you have found a date that suits everyone and is available for the ceremony and reception, don't forget to book! Ask if you can make a provisional booking first, say for the ceremony, while you check that your reception venue is also available.

BOOKING VENUES

✔ Do try to book as far ahead as possible. This will give you a much wider choice.

✔ Do agree a price or fees.

✔ Do make sure you have written confirmation of dates, times and charges.

✔ Do tell everyone essential to the wedding the date, time and place.

AVAILABILITY INFORMATION

Preferred season ....

Special dates ....

Dates to avoid: Bride ....

                Groom ....

Impossible dates for other people (parents, best man, bridesmaids, ushers, special guests) ....

....

....

Ceremony venue available ....

....

Reception venue available ....

....

Availability of photographer, florist and other key players

....

VENUE CONFIRMATION

	Address	Date	Time	Confirmed
Ceremony	....	....	....	☐
	....			
	....			
Reception	....	....	....	☐
	....			
	....			
Honeymoon	....	....		☐
	....			
	....			

Wedding address book

A good idea is to start a wedding address book where you file contact numbers, ideas and any useful articles you may read. This can cover everything from information about dress and hair styles, wedding cakes, unusual receptions, gifts, place settings and decorations, to ideas for your future home. Note down and keep anything which might be helpful for the months ahead. It is a good idea to divide your file into sections such as Dresses, Music, Food and Menus, Shoes, Reception, Invitations, Flowers, and so on. This way, you can access information easily without having to wade through all your other entries.

Some stationery companies such as Smythson, tel: 020 7629 8558, or Smythson By Post, tel: 020 7318 1515, sell special wedding notebooks which are already divided into useful sections.

The internet is a useful tool for fact-finding, giving information on a range of services, including clothes, transport, finance, music and flowers, and general help with everything from planning, making speeches, etiquette and finding the perfect venue, to organising the honeymoon. Good sites to try include:

- www.all-about-weddings.co.uk
- www.qm4.com
- www.wedding-service.co.uk
- www.weddings.co.uk
- www.webweddings.co.uk
- www.WeddingGuideUk.com

5 KEY ROLES

Careful organisation can ensure all your wedding plans go smoothly and help to avoid last-minute panics.

Always remember that you can't do everything yourself. This applies especially to the bride and groom. Naturally, you want everything to be absolutely perfect for your wedding day, but if the bride or groom wear themselves out trying to sort out every single potential problem, there's not much chance of them being on top form for the big day. Organisation is the key.

Most couples choose to have a best man, bridesmaids or other attendants, whether they are having a civil or a religious wedding. As well as adding to the fun of the day, it is also a way of sharing out some of the responsibilities beforehand, during the ceremony and afterwards at the reception. Planning a wedding can take a great deal of time, organisation and hard work, and when you are deciding who to ask it is important to pick people who you enjoy being with and who you can rely on.

This section is a guide to the key roles, who does

what and, traditionally, what is expected of everyone. Basically, it tells you how to be the perfect…

Bride

This is your big day and all the major decisions revolve around you. Traditionally the bride decides everything, including the type of wedding ceremony, the date and time, hymns and music, the reception venue, food and wines. In practice, the bride and groom usually make these decisions together. It is an important day for both of you and the groom should not feel like a guest at his own wedding. Even if you are paying for the day yourselves, discuss plans with your parents as it is a special day for them too.

Each of your key duties should be discussed with your fiancé, except your choice of wedding dress. Don't forget that mothers, sisters and bridesmaids will be only too willing to help.

KEY DUTIES – BRIDE

- Decide on the type of ceremony, date and time
- Choose any hymns and music
- Organise the wedding party – choose a chief bridesmaid, bridesmaids and attendants
- Set the date for the wedding rehearsal
- Draw up a guest list with both sets of parents
- Find the perfect reception venue and decide on style, colour scheme or theme

- Organise music or entertainment at the reception
- Choose a menu
- Choose wedding stationery
- Contact any guests who have failed to reply to invitations and finalise the guest list
- Work out a seating plan and keep the reception venue/caterers informed
- Find a wedding dress, going-away outfit, bridesmaids' and attendants' clothes, plus all accessories, and arrange hairstyles and beauty preparations
- Order wedding cake
- Find a florist and order flowers
- Book photographer
- Draw up a wedding gift list and write thank-yous for gifts
- Send out change-of-address cards
- Notify organisations and authorities of any name change
- Act as general coordinator
- Find time for yourself and your fiancé

THE BRIDE

✔ Do take into account the feelings of your family.
✔ Do smile and enjoy yourself.
✔ Do make the most of every moment.
✘ Don't let the planning become too stressful.
✘ Don't forget you can't please everyone.
✘ Don't forget the meaning of the whole event.

Groom

Traditionally the groom is responsible for all the legal and financial aspects of getting married and he makes any payments due for the wedding ceremony. Most grooms nowadays take a more active role in the planning. One groom recently described marriage preparations as being like a multiple-choice exam paper, with various acceptable options being presented by his fiancée and her mother for his final decision. Alternatively, it may be that the groom takes on overall responsibility for a particular aspect, such as the catering or music. Whatever you decide, it is important that both bride and groom feel completely happy with their wedding day.

KEY DUTIES – GROOM

- Organise the registrar and pay fees
- Pay church fees, including banns, marriage service, choir, organist, bell-ringers (either these should be paid before the wedding or the money should be given to the best man to pay on the day)
- Choose a best man and ushers
- Find a wedding suit and going-away outfit and make sure hair is cut
- Buy wedding rings
- Choose attendants' gifts
- Organise car or other transport for bride and groom after the ceremony

- Make second speech at the reception
- Arrange and book the honeymoon
- Organise any necessary vaccinations and ensure passports are valid

THE GROOM

✔ Do think about the meaning of the words as you exchange vows.

✘ Don't forget it's your day and you should enjoy it.

Find useful information at:
- **www.webweddings.co.uk**

Bride's mother

The bride's mother is the wedding host. She is traditionally responsible for the organisation of the reception and her duties overlap with those of the bride. Although the bride chooses the style of decorations and the wedding cake and flowers, it is usually her mother who attends to the details, makes sure the cake is delivered on time and that everything runs according to plan.

KEY DUTIES – BRIDE'S MOTHER

- Arrange press announcements
- Draw up guest list with the bride and groom, and groom's parents

- Order stationery (with bride and groom)
- Send out wedding invitations and list responses –
  all replies are addressed to her
- Draw up a seating plan together with bride and groom
- Choose an outfit and help bride choose wedding dress
  and bridesmaids' dresses
- Organise flowers with the bride
- Choose and book a photographer with the bride
- Arrange transport for the bridal party
- Order and arrange delivery of the wedding cake
- Order and arrange table settings and decorations, plus
  any extras, like candles
- Arrange a changing room for the bride and groom after
  the reception
- Help organise overnight accommodation for guests if
  needed
- Help dress the bride on the wedding day
- Make sure the ushers have the order of service sheets
- Ensure the best man has the buttonholes
- Form the receiving line and greet guests at the reception
- Arrange a display of gifts and take charge of the
  wedding gifts after the wedding
- Take charge of the cake and send slices to anyone
  unable to attend
- Collect proofs of the photographs and take orders to
  pass to the photographer
- Collect and distribute the wedding photographs.

As you can see from the list of duties, the bride's mother works hard behind the scenes. She is traditionally the last to leave the reception, making sure that guests have left safely and the clearing up is organised.

Bride's father

The father of the bride travels to the church with his daughter and 'gives her away'. If this is impossible for any reason, an older brother or uncle usually steps into this role, but there is no reason why the bride cannot choose a female relative or friend or even her mother, and this is no longer uncommon.

KEY DUTIES – BRIDE'S FATHER

- Set budget (if appropriate and he is funding the wedding)
- Organise a wedding suit
- Accompany bride to the ceremony
- Give away bride during the ceremony
- Arrive early at the reception with the bride's mother as joint host
- Form part of receiving line to greet guests
- Ask the minister (if it is a church wedding) to say grace at the reception
- Make the first speech and propose the first toast – the convention now is for the bride's father to make the first speech at the reception, but traditionally the speech was always made by another male from the bride's family or her party and her father did not speak.

Useful websites:
• **www.weddings.co.uk** (section on mens' clothes)
• **www.webweddings.co.uk** (advice for speeches)

Best man

The best man plays a vital role supporting the groom. He is usually a brother or close friend and he should be responsible, level-headed and reliable. He should liaise with the bride's family, know exactly what the plans are and help the groom with practical arrangements.

KEY DUTIES – BEST MAN

• Keep in close contact with the bride's family to help with organisation

• Arrange a stag night and make sure the groom gets home safely

• Attend wedding rehearsal

• Organise overnight accommodation for himself and the groom on the night before the wedding if necessary

• On the wedding morning check that the groom has all the necessary documents – certificates, licences, passports, visas, tickets, cases packed, wedding clothes and rings

• Telephone the bride's parents to wish them well, check on any last-minute hitches and remind bride's father to bring along any messages from absent guests

• Make sure buttonholes and order of service sheets are collected or delivered to the church ready for the ushers to hand out to guests

- Check ushers know what they should be doing
- Arrange for the groom's going-away clothes to be left at the reception on the wedding morning or the day before and look after the groom's luggage
- Make sure the groom arrives for the ceremony on time and arrange any transport needed
- Pay any fees that have not already been settled by the groom
- Finalise parking arrangements for the ceremony and reception
- Organise transport for the bride and groom after the reception
- Look after the ring(s) until the exchange during the ceremony
- Pass the ring(s) to the minister or groom at the appropriate point in the ceremony
- Make sure all guests have transport from the ceremony to the reception
- Sometimes take part in the receiving line, greeting guests and helping to make sure everyone enjoys themselves
- Liaise with the toastmaster or announce the speeches and cake-cutting himself
- Make the third speech and thank the groom for his toast to the bridesmaids
- Read out any cards or messages from absent guests
- Agree time when the bride and groom should go off to change prior to leaving
- Look after the groom's clothes if he changes to go away, and return any hired suits

On the day the best man should carry an emergency kit, including:

- Mobile phone or cash for telephone
- Emergency telephone numbers, including taxi firm, photographer, etc.
- Spare place-name cards
- Spare order of service sheets
- Headache pills
- Handkerchief
- Plasters and safety pins
- Spare cash and credit cards for emergencies
- Umbrellas

Should anything go wrong on the day, the bride and groom should not have to do any running around to sort it out. The best man is there as a troubleshooter as well as for moral support for the groom and he should be capable of organising help from ushers or others as required.

Although not essential, it is also often the best man who plots any 'decoration' of the going-away car. If he is in charge of this, he might also include a cleaning kit to pack in the groom's car.

Useful websites:
- **www.thebestman.com**
- **www.webweddings.co.uk** (excellent section on speeches)

Chief bridesmaid

Many brides choose small nieces or goddaughters as bridesmaids but you also really need a friend and confidante throughout the months of planning, someone who will cheer you up when it all seems too much and who will tell you, truthfully, what she thinks of the dress you are considering. The chief bridesmaid, or matron of honour if she is married, is usually a best friend, sister or cousin.

She generally helps the bride with the wedding preparations and on the day, and is the bride's equivalent of a best man.

KEY DUTIES – CHIEF BRIDESMAID

- Help the bride to choose her wedding dress
- Help find bridesmaids' outfits, including her own – she may pay for her own dress if it is something she can wear on other occasions
- Arrange a hen party
- Attend the wedding rehearsal
- Help the bride to dress on the wedding day
- Wait at the ceremony for the bride and her father to arrive and supervise any young bridesmaids or page boys
- Help to rearrange the bride's veil and, if there is one, hold her train before the bride begins the procession up the aisle

- Take the bride's bouquet at the chancel steps
- Take charge of the bride's bouquet during the service and then carry it into the vestry for the signing of the register (the chief bridesmaid walks alongside the best man into the vestry)
- Return bouquet to the bride after the signing of the register for the bride to carry in the procession back down the aisle
- Leave the church with the best man following the bride and groom
- Help the bride into her car when she leaves for the reception
- Sometimes take part in the receiving line to greet guests and generally mix with guests
- Look after bride's bouquet at the reception until the bride is about to leave
- Check bride's going-away outfit and luggage are ready
- Take charge of the bride's dress when she leaves
- Help bride's mother with any clearing away after the reception

On the day the chief bridesmaid should have an emergency kit safely stowed somewhere out of sight but accessible, including:

- Comb, brush, hairclips, hairspray, make-up and mirror
- Perfume
- Toothpaste and toothbrush

- Safety pins, needle and thread
- Spare pair of stockings or tights
- Headache pills, antacid
- Antihistamine cream or tablets if the bride is prone to allergies
- Plasters
- Tampons, pads
- Wet wipes, tissues
- Sun block if it is summer and you will be out of doors
- Hard-boiled sweets, in case of coughs
- Clear nail varnish to halt runs in stockings and tights
- Copies of maps and directions
- Phone numbers for all service companies
- Mobile phone or cash for telephone
- Bottle of water

Other bridesmaids

Traditionally, the role of the bridesmaids was to protect the bride from evil and help her to dress when she was thought to be at her most vulnerable.

Bridesmaids were always unmarried attendants and at one time would have been chosen from among the bride's and groom's sisters. Now, they are often friends or may be young nieces, goddaughters or the daughters of friends. If they are very young, they will need looking after on the day.

KEY DUTIES – BRIDESMAID

- Help choose their outfits
- Help the bride with her dress, veil and train before and after the ceremony
- Form part of the procession following the chief bridesmaid
- Follow the chief bridesmaid and best man out of the church after the signing of the register
- Travel with the best man and chief bridesmaid to the reception
- Help with drinks at the reception if asked
- Offer slices of wedding cake to guests

Usher

Ushers are normally chosen from the family and friends of both the bride and the groom, although traditionally it is the groom who does the choosing. Their duties are really confined to the wedding day and more specifically to the ceremony. They should be kept informed of any specific seating instructions or plans and advised of any elderly or disabled guests who may need special help. Ushers are really needed only for church weddings and, depending on the size of the wedding, there should be at least three.

KEY DUTIES – USHER
- Before the wedding meet the best man and both families to discuss arrangements
- Arrive first at church to direct guests to their seats. The bride's family and guests sit on the left of the aisle and the groom's on the right
- Organise parking
- Hand out order of service sheets, or hymn and prayer books to guests as they arrive
- Distribute buttonholes as arranged
- Escort the bride's mother to the front left pew
- Escort the groom's parents to their pew near the front behind the groom and best man's seats
- Gather guests together for photographs
- Make sure guests have transport to the reception

Page boy

Page boys are not essential but a bride may choose a young nephew or friend's son to be a page boy.

KEY DUTIES – PAGE BOY
- Take part in the procession and recession along the aisle following the bridesmaids
- Wear an outfit chosen by the bride (and look cute)
- Wait at the chancel steps or sit during the signing of the register

Flower girl

There is no necessity for a bride to choose a flower girl but if she does, because they are usually quite little, they would not have to stand with the other bridesmaids during the service.

KEY DUTIES – FLOWER GIRL

- A flower girl could be asked to carry a basket of rose petals in twists of tissue paper or cones made from photocopied sheets of music which she should hand out to guests to throw instead of confetti, if allowed by the church or registrar

Guest

Guests have responsibilities too!

KEY DUTIES – GUEST

- Reply promptly to the invitation
- Dress appropriately on the day – if there is no dress code, it is usual to dress smartly
- Choose a wedding present – from the gift list or your own choice if you know the couple well enough to select something they would like (if you are unable to attend the ceremony, it is not essential to give a present)
- Arrive on time for the ceremony
- Turn off your mobile phone before the ceremony – they have a habit of ringing just as the minister asks if there is any just cause or impediment to the marriage

- If you have small children with you, take them outside if they are noisy during the ceremony – however welcome they are, it is important that the service should be audible to everyone
- Keep phones switched off for the speeches at the reception
- Don't heckle – even if the speeches are lengthy
- Congratulate the groom and parents, but give your best wishes to the bride
- Write a thank-you note to the wedding hosts

6 WEDDING COSTS

Traditionally, the burden of paying for a daughter's wedding fell on the bride's father, but conventions change. Today, more than half the couples marrying pay for their own weddings, and most contribute something. Often the groom's family also offers to pay for a specific part of the wedding, such as champagne and drinks at the reception, and godparents or other close relatives may also like to help.

The average cost of a wedding today is about £15,000. Of course, you don't have to spend as much as that and it is possible to get married for as little as £62.50 in a register office if you wish.

Setting a budget
Before you make any definite arrangements, and certainly before you start spending any money, you must set a budget. Be ruthlessly honest about what you can afford. There is no point in having an extravagantly lavish wedding day if you are still paying for it for the first years of your married life together.

- Work out your available budget

- How much money do you have saved and available?

- How much are parents willing to contribute?

- Will you have any extra savings by the wedding day?

To work out the costs you are likely to incur, find out what you need to spend.

WEDDING COSTS	
	£
Engagement ring	....
Bride's wedding ring	....
Groom's wedding ring	....
Church/registrar fees	....
Music	....
Flowers	....
(for the ceremony, reception, buttonholes, bridesmaids' posies)	
Bride's bouquet	....
Invitations and stationery	....
Wedding dress	....
Headdress and veil	....
Shoes and accessories	....
Groom's clothes	....
Attendants' outfits	....
Going-away outfit	....
Special lingerie	....
Cosmetics	....
Photographs	....

Video	....
Wedding cars and transport	....
Reception venue	....
Catering	....
Drinks	....
Wedding cake	....
Wedding-night hotel	....
Honeymoon	....
Insurance	....
Miscellaneous (including gifts for attendants, favours, etc.)	....
Total	_____

A limited budget does not have to mean a dull wedding. There are ways to cut costs, and style costs nothing. Friends and family may be able to help with food or drink, bridesmaids' dresses or flowers. A friend may be able to offer a classic sports car to drive you from the ceremony, and a grandparent may have a house or garden big enough to hold the reception.

Always decide what is essential for you and make that a priority, then make savings on other elements which are less important.

If you are on a tight budget it is better to limit the number of guests than cut down on the quality and quantity of the food and drink. Few guests will remember the splendid vintage car or the bouquet, but they will remember going home hungry.

Who pays for what

Traditionally…the bride's parents pay for:

- National press announcements
- Invitations and stationery
- Wedding clothes and accessories for the bride and bridesmaids or attendants
- Flowers for the church and reception
- The photographer
- Transport to the ceremony and afterwards for the bridal party
- The reception
- The wedding cake

The groom pays for:

- Announcements in the local press
- The cost of the church or register office
- Marriage certificate
- Bouquets for the brides and bridesmaids, floral corsages for both mothers and buttonholes for himself, best man and ushers
- Engagement and wedding rings
- Transport from the ceremony for himself and the bride
- Presents for the best man and attendants
- The honeymoon

Quotations, estimates and deposits

Contact a range of companies to check on costs. When you have made your choice, always ask for a quotation rather than an estimate.

A quotation is a set price for supplying a service or goods, whereas an estimate gives only a general idea of the final cost and this could be subject to market fluctuations in price.

Some suppliers insist on a deposit as part-payment in advance. This confirms your booking and is usually non-returnable in the event of a cancellation.

Insurance

A great deal of money is spent on arranging a wedding, not forgetting the time and effort involved, and it may be worth thinking about insurance. There are specific wedding policies which cover things such as theft of presents, damage to the wedding dress and public liability should a guest be injured and press for damages. Policies usually cover the loss of deposits due to the cancellation of the wedding and may even offer compensation or cover the cost of rebooking if, say, the reception venue was suddenly shut.

Contact several companies and ask for quotes before taking out a policy and also contact your home contents insurance company. *Always* read any small print and check what is actually covered.

COMPANIES OFFERING WEDDING INSURANCE

Country Mutual Insurance Brokers: 0118 957 5491

Ecclesiastical Direct: 0800 336622

E&L Insurance Services: 0870 742 3700

Traveller's Protection Services: 01603 767699

Wedding coordinators

There are a growing number of wedding coordinators or organisers – individuals or companies who will help you organise your wedding. Starting with the stationery, they offer advice on every aspect of planning. If you want a particular colour scheme or theme to your day, they will ensure everything falls smoothly into place.

WEDDING COORDINATORS

✔ Do ask friends for personal recommendations and check fees (you should expect to pay around £800 for the service).

✘ Don't employ a wedding coordinator who asks you to come to see her. They should always come to you.

WEDDING COORDINATORS AND ORGANISERS

Alternative Occasions: 01932 872115

Patricia Rogerson: 07771 655996

The Kodak Wedding Information Service: 0800 783 7452 (for comprehensive listings), or

● **www.kodakweddings.com**

Budget planners

There are now several internet companies specialising in everything to do with weddings. They offer advice and ideas and are a good place to source everything from gifts to wedding dresses, travel to wedding venues.

They also help with planning, including personalised to-do lists and budget planners, and will even send out reminders for what you should be doing at key points in the countdown to your wedding.

Good ones to try are:
• www.confetti.co.uk
• www.hitched.co.uk
• www.all-about-weddings.co.uk
• www.qm4.com

Cost-cutting tips

It is cheaper to get married between October and March and on weekdays, when there are fewer weddings and you have a better chance of bargaining. Honeymoons may cost less too.

You can save money by having your wedding dress made by a dressmaker. Study bride magazines to find styles you like. Alternatively, you could hire a dress or look for a second-hand one – some have never been worn (not always for sad reasons).

- Buy bridesmaids' dresses from high street shops. There are lots of pretty styles and you can individualise them by adding flowers and accessories.

- Save money on insurance – check whether wedding gifts are covered by your home contents insurance policy.

- Design and make your own place cards, order of service sheets and even invitations (some of the internet wedding companies can help).

- Remember, a buffet is usually less expensive than a sit-down meal at the reception.

- Consider a venue that allows you to provide your own food or drink or to hire a private firm of caterers.

- Transform a plain reception venue with flowers, fabric drapes, garlands, candles and decorations. Be creative. Bride and home interior magazines are good sources of inspiration.

- You can make a huge saving by holding the reception at either of your parents' homes or that of a willing relative.

- Limit the number of hired wedding cars or ask a friend with a special car to lend it to you for the day.

- Make sure the photographer knows exactly what shots you want and limit the number taken (you

usually pay for a specified number). Always get a
written quote.

- Place cheap, disposable cameras on tables for
  guests to take informal photos.
- If you want a wedding video, you could ask a friend
  to do the filming for you, though you may not be
  that pleased with the results.
- Musical friends may be more than happy to play
  or sing at your reception.

7 INVITATIONS & WEDDING STATIONERY

Drawing up your guest list should be one of the first things you do. It is important to decide who you want to invite, who you really ought to invite and who you absolutely have to invite, and you should do this in consultation with both sets of parents. Traditionally, a third of the invitations were always for the bride's family, a third for the groom's and a third for the bride and groom. To be fair, whoever is paying for the bulk of the wedding should have the final say on numbers.

The groom's mother should send the bride's mother the names and addresses of guests she would like invited and as a courtesy an invitation should be sent to the groom's family.

WEDDING GUESTS
✓ Do check guest lists with both sets of in-laws.
✓ Do give yourselves plenty of time to compile your list.
✓ Do check that your reception venue can accommodate all your guests before finalising your list.
✓ Do double-check your lists.

✘ Don't forget anyone vital. Invite all close family members. You may forget them, but they will remember you.

Choosing your stationery

There is a range of styles to match all tastes and budgets available from good stationers, specialist companies, department stores and local printers. They should all carry samples they can show or send you. Invitations can help to set the tone for your wedding, so don't be afraid to be creative.

For a formal wedding, traditional invitations are simple, high-quality white or cream paper or card. Ideally, they should be engraved on one side only in black lettering. Engraving is the most expensive form of printing but it gives the best raised-print effect. Other options include thermographic and flat printing.

Engraved or printed invitations are usually the most convenient for anything other than a very small wedding. When choosing stationery, ask to see examples of different typefaces, as changing the type can make an enormous difference to the appearance of your invites. Personalised wedding stationery can include:

• Invitations and envelopes
• Invitation reply cards

- Menus and place-name cards
- Cake boxes (with greaseproof lining)
- Engagement party invitations
- Napkins and napkin rings
- Wedding notebooks
- Change-of-address cards
- Bridal notepaper and envelopes
- Thank-you cards and envelopes
- Luggage labels
- Matchbooks or boxes and drink mats
- Keepsake books with pre-printed layouts to display such items as press announcements, guest lists, order of service sheets and replies
- Guest book or album for guests to sign at the reception
- Photograph albums
- Order of service sheets (always check with your minister or registrar before printing)

Check major department stores and good stationers for their range of wedding stationery. Also look on the internet. The usual wedding websites often have suggestions or special offers. Also try:

- **www.paperalchemy.com** which carries a wide range of products as well as offering design tips. You can even choose wax seals, ribbons and rose petals to personalise your stationery.

It is also possible to send out personalised e-invitations. Check out:

• **www.bluemountain.com**

Engagement party invitations

Most stationers sell ready-printed party invitations but you may prefer to have your own printed.

FORMAL INVITATION

Mr and Mrs Frank Smith
request the pleasure
of the company of

....

at a party to celebrate
the engagement of their daughter Lucy
to Mr Joseph Cook on

...............(date)...............

at 8.30 pm at .... (venue).............

Mrs Frank Williams
(address).............RSVP

LESS FORMAL OPTIONS

To..

Please join us to celebrate Lucy's engagement to Joe Cook

on............................

Lucy Williams and Joe Cook

invite you to a party to celebrate their engagement.

Date....................
Place....................
Time....................

For practical help with planning parties, check the internet. Both **www.confetti.co.uk/parties** and **www.hitched.co.uk** have tips and advice on throwing the perfect party and may offer special deals on wine, beer and invitations, for instance.

WEDDING INVITATIONS

Invitations are sent from whoever is acting as hosts for the wedding and the wording varies according to the situation. Most people now request the 'pleasure' rather than the 'honour' of a guest's company. There are no strict rules about wording, but most invitations usually follow a similar format.

BRIDE'S PARENTS AS HOSTS

Mr and Mrs William Jones
request the pleasure of the company of

....

at the marriage of their daughter Elizabeth
to Mr Alexander Shaw

at All Soul's Church, Lichfield
on Saturday 4 November 2000 at 2.30 pm

and afterwards at Wye Cross Hall, Lichfield

RSVP
(Address here)

The guest's name would be handwritten at the top left-hand corner on the next example.

Mr and Mrs William Jones
request the pleasure of your company
at the marriage of their daughter Elizabeth

to Mr Alexander Shaw

at All Soul's Church, Lichfield
on Saturday 4 November 2000
at 2.30 pm

and afterwards at Wye Cross Hall,
Lichfield

RSVP
(Address here)

Invitation variations

Bridal couple as hosts:

Elizabeth Jones and Alex Shaw
request the pleasure of your company at their marriage
at…

Remarried mother as host with stepfather:
Mr and Mrs Nicholas Wright
request the pleasure of your company at the marriage
of her daughter…

Bride's mother as host if she is divorced:
Mrs Alice Jones
requests the pleasure of your company at the marriage
of her daughter…

Bride's mother as host if she is widowed:
Mrs William Jones
requests the pleasure of your company at the marriage
of her daughter…

Divorced parents as hosts:
Mr William Jones and Mrs Alice Jones
request the pleasure of your company at the marriage
of their daughter…

Divorced parents as hosts if bride's mother has
remarried:
Mr William Jones and Mrs Nicholas Wright
request the pleasure of your company at the marriage
of their daughter…

Bride's father as host:
Mr William Jones
requests the pleasure of your company at the marriage
of his daughter…

Remarried father as host with stepmother:
Mr and Mrs William Jones
request the pleasure of your company at the marriage
of his daughter…

When the hosts are a different relation to the bride:
Mr and Mrs Ben Arnold
request the pleasure of your company at the marriage
of their niece…

If there is no family connection:
Mr and Mrs Michael Clarke
request the pleasure of your company at the
marriage of
Elizabeth Jones to Mr Alexander Shaw

Without the name of the hosts:
The pleasure of your company is requested at the
marriage of
Miss Elizabeth Jones to Mr Alexander Shaw

If the wedding ceremony is to take place in a register
office or small chapel where space is limited, it may
be impossible for all the guests to attend, in which
case reception-only invitations should be sent out,
possibly with an explanatory note.

RECEPTION ONLY INVITATION

Mr and Mrs William Jones

request the pleasure of
your company at a reception

at Wye Cross Hall, Lichfield
on Saturday 4 November 2000
at 4 pm

following the marriage
of their daughter

Elizabeth

to Mr Alexander Shaw

RSVP

(Address here)

This could also be amended to invite guests to an evening reception only.

With double weddings, if two couples are to be married together, the older couple is mentioned first. In the case of, for instance, a daughter and niece, the daughter would come first as she has the closer relationship to the hosts.

Extra information

Some people include a pre-printed reply card with their invitations but this is not necessary, although it may encourage swifter replies. It is a good idea to send any maps or directions, with parking spaces marked, together with any details of places to stay overnight that guests might find helpful. This could include hotels, guest houses, B&Bs or names of friends and relations who have offered accommodation. Train times and telephone numbers for local taxis can also be useful.

You can make it clear that children are being invited by including their names on the invitation to their parents. You might also choose to give guests an idea of what to expect – dinner, buffet, dancing. If you wish guests to follow a specific dress code, this should be printed in the bottom right-hand corner of the invitation. For instance, for a dance or disco you may want guests to wear black tie or evening dress to the ceremony, in which case you would print 'Black tie'. You should also let the minister know.

Addressing the invitations

Guests' names should be handwritten in ink either on the top left-hand corner of the invitation or in the space provided by the wording. Envelopes should also be addressed by hand.

For a married couple, the names should be written Mr and Mrs Richard Webb; for a family, Mr and Mrs Richard Webb, Lauren and Jack. Couples in long-term relationships should be invited as a couple, regardless of how well you know the partner.

As a courtesy, the minister and his wife should be invited and invitations should also be sent to any close friends or relatives that you already know are unable to attend.

Invitation replies

When guests begin to reply, keep a detailed list. You will need this to draw up a final guest list to inform the reception venue and caterers of numbers and to work out a seating plan. You could draw up a table as shown below.

	Invitation Sent (Date)	Bride/ Groom's guest	Accommodation needed
Name Address Tel/email			
Name Address Tel/email			

INVITATIONS CHECKLIST

Ask for quotes for all possible choices of
invitations and typefaces ☐

Shop around and compare quotes ☐

Make sure the price includes envelopes ☐

Type the exact wording you want for your invitations,
then check and double-check before giving the
typed sheet to your printer ☐

Order your invitations at least three months before
the wedding (they can take a month to be printed) ☐

Arrange a collection date well before you need
to send them ☐

Ask to see a proof of the invitation before it is printed
and read carefully for errors. You should check paper
quality and colour, as well as details – such as names,
addresses, dates and telephone numbers, spelling,
punctuation and typeface ☐

Check the invitations again carefully for printing errors
before sending them out (ask someone else to read
through as well) ☐

Order extra invitations to allow for mistakes when
addressing them and for last-minute additions to
the guest list ☐

Send the invitations out eight weeks before the
wedding (or twelve weeks if the wedding is at a
particularly busy time of year) ☐

ORDER OF SERVICE SHEETS

Ushers normally hand guests an order of service sheet as they arrive at the church for the wedding ceremony. You may feel there are sufficient hymn and prayer books and that special sheets are unnecessary, but they do make it easier to follow the service and mean that guests know exactly what is happening and when to stand or sit. They are another way to personalise your day and also give you the chance to name and credit readers and musicians.

ORDER OF SERVICE SHEETS

✓ Do consult your minister about your choices of music and readings before you go ahead with printing.

✓ Do check copyright. Copyright holders are usually listed in any printed book and they should always be contacted before you reproduce any words in print – either for hymns or for readings. It may be sufficient to print an acknowledgement or you may have to pay a small fee.

Most companies will be able to show you sample sheets and there will usually be a step-by-step form for you to fill in all the details.

Order of service sheets may include:

• Names of the bride and groom
• Name of the church and minister

- Name of the organist and choir
- Names of readers and any solo musicians
- Date and time of the ceremony
- Titles and composers of any music played
- Processional music – as bride arrives
- Recessional music – as bride and groom leave
- Music played or sung during the register signing
- Prayers and responses
- Marriage service
- Two or three hymns – with full text
- Readings – these may be printed in full or just state the chapter and verse, or title

You can find suggestions for hymns, music and readings in Chapter 18.

8 THE RECEPTION

Once the ceremony is over and the bride and groom are now officially husband and wife, it is time to celebrate. A feast has long been the traditional wedding celebration and is an important part of the ritual that everyone should enjoy. It gives guests the opportunity to congratulate the couple and toast their happiness, and the newlyweds the chance to relax and meet old friends and relations.

The style of the reception is up to you, though you may want it to reflect the style and tone of your wedding ceremony. The choice is usually made by the bride and groom, in consultation with parents if they are contributing, and it is important to set a budget at the outset and stick to it. There are numerous factors which come into play when calculating your budget but, while they will vary from one type of wedding to another, the basics will always be roughly the same.

There are many different approaches to marriage celebrations and while the only two essential ingredients are champagne and a wedding cake, reception menus range from drinks with canapés, through buffets, light wedding breakfasts and afternoon tea, to elaborate sit-down meals.

A sit-down meal will probably be more expensive than a buffet or canapés, and cheapest of all is to ask friends and family to cater for you, although it is better to avoid this unless you are certain they are up to the challenge. Providing for your guests should be a priority, especially as many will have travelled long distances to be with you. Try not to ask more than you can properly cater for.

Choosing a reception venue

The choice of where to hold your reception is endless – from church halls to stately homes, London Zoo to your own home, grand hotels to marquees, and countless other unusual locations, including museums, galleries, film studios, theme parks and battleships.

It is a good idea to take the wedding venue into account when you make your choice to avoid the problem of guests having to travel too far from ceremony to reception; and now there are so many approved wedding premises, it may be possible to combine your ceremony and party at the same venue.

RECEPTION VENUES
✔ Do listen to recommendations.
✔ Do go and visit anywhere you are considering.

✔ Do make sure they can accommodate your specific plans and requirements.

✔ Do book at least three months in advance.

✔ Do look at menus if catering is part of the package.

✔ Do look at costs.

✘ Don't pay a deposit until you are sure – your money is unlikely to be refunded if you change your mind.

Timing

When deciding on the type of reception, do consider the time of day it will be held. If your wedding is early afternoon, guests will probably eat before the ceremony and will not want a heavy meal. Likewise, if your reception is at midday, lunch is probably essential.

Booking

Popular venues may be reserved months ahead, so always book as early as possible. Always check what exactly is covered in the price and, especially if catering and decorating are included, check exactly what is offered.

Always ask for written confirmation and keep the manager informed about the number of guests coming – *not* just the number you have invited. You will be expected to pay for all the food ordered, even if some guests do not turn up, though normally you will be charged only for the drink consumed.

When searching for your perfect venue, there are a number of issues that need to be addressed.

RECEPTION VENUE CHECKLIST

Availability ☐

Parking facilities and access ☐

Distance from the ceremony ☐

Does it have a licence for alcohol? ☐

Does the venue provide catering? ☐

Are you allowed to use your own caterers? ☐

Do you have to buy drinks from the venue? ☐

Are drinks supplied on a sale-or-return basis? ☐

Can you supply your own; is there a corkage charge? ☐

What time does it close? ☐

What facilities are there for music? ☐

What is the policy on musicians/bands/discos? ☐

If the reception will be partly outdoors, what if it rains? ☐

Exactly what is included in the quote? ☐

You should also check:
Yellow Pages
The National Trust: 020 7222 9251 (who should be able to supply you with a list of local options).

Also, websites such as:

- www.confetti.co.uk
- www.hitched.co.uk
- www.all-about-weddings.co.uk
- www.wedding-service.co.uk
- www.weddings.co.uk
- www.webweddings.co.uk

Decorations

The style of decoration you choose for your reception may well be dictated by where it is being held. Ideas that would work well in a city hotel would look out of place in a medieval hall, and a light silvery colour scheme might just seem stark and chilly on a gloomy winter's day.

Sometimes the venue staff or caterers will organise all the table and other decorations, but this is usually after consultation with the bride or bride's mother and you should say, early on, if there is an overall colour scheme to the wedding or any other theme. If the reception is to be held in a hall, you need to check that you can have access early that morning to arrange everything.

Whether you are responsible for the decorations or someone else is arranging them for you, there are several things to consider.

You may want a colour theme to the reception, possibly to complement your own dress and those of the bridesmaids, the flowers you have chosen or the season of the year. You might also want the colours to fit in with an overall 'look'.

Classically traditional A creamy-white colour scheme, roses and other traditional flowers and foliage, crisp white napkins, crystal glasses and simple place cards.

Contemporary With sculptural flowers such as arum lilies and grasses in simple, stylish arrangements. Napkins could be tied with ornamental grass or ivy and place names could be written on leaves, or labels, tied to single flowers or bamboo stems laid across each plate.

Romantic This look can easily be achieved with soft, pretty colours and lots of flowers, bowls of floating candles and petals, napkins tied with ribbons or sprigs of lavender, and tall, chunky candles standing in floral circlets. Scatter lavender or tiny, fragrant rosebuds or petals across the tables.

Informal For a relaxed modern look, use brighter colours for flowers, napkins and glasses. Fruit can look effective among flowers and trailing leaves, and boldly coloured candles or holders and sparkling table confetti all add to the mood.

Midwinter wedding For a warm, opulent winter wedding, use richer textures like velvets and brocades and stronger colours. Try baroque reds, purples, burgundies, shades of gold and terracotta, deep blues and green. Flower arrangements can be dramatic, with deep-coloured roses and amaryllis, twisted willow twigs and trailing leaves. If possible, light log fires and candles.

Dramatic evening reception Line the roof of a marquee with midnight blue or black fabric and cover with twinkling fairy lights to create the illusion of a starry night sky.

ACHIEVING THE DESIRED LOOK

✔ Do look at table settings and glasses – even the most standard hotel china can be personalised.

✔ Do consider which flowers would add to the atmosphere you are trying to create and think about varieties that are available at the time of your wedding.

✔ Do think about extra touches that could add to the mood, such as candles, balloons, favours, crackers, wedding bubbles or other wedding keepsakes.

✔ Do be creative.

You can find out more about choosing flowers in Chapter 11.

Bride magazines are good sources of inspiration. They often have novel, contemporary suggestions, as well as the names of specific suppliers.

Call Walking on Water Creative Events, tel: 020 8438 0050, for imaginative transformations of your reception venue.

Receptions at home and in marquees

Some receptions are held at home, either to cut costs or because parents or a close relative have a particularly beautiful home or garden which will make a stunning setting for a wedding party. Some couples simply prefer the idea of a reception at home because of the freedom and the intimate friendly atmosphere that can be created.

Gardens provide a different scene and are wonderful for summer drinks, but as the weather is often unpredictable some couples choose to hire a marquee. This gives flexibility, providing extra room and shelter if it is cold and raining, and shade if it is too sunny. Guests will still be able to go outside if the garden is large enough and the sides of some marquees can be opened out. However, they can be expensive to hire.

Drinks and canapés or a buffet meal may work best at home, depending on the space available, how formal or informal you want the reception to be and how many guests are invited. It is also perfectly possible for the wedding party to have a meal together, with a larger party for guests at home later.

RECEPTIONS AT HOME

✔ Do let neighbours know what you are planning.

✔ Do consider where guests are going to park – in some areas this could be a real problem.

If you are having a firm of caterers they should be able to supply you with everything from tables and chairs to cutlery and napkins, *but* if you are catering yourselves, you will have to organise everything you need.

Catering

The most foolproof way of finding a good caterer is by word of mouth…or tasting their food for yourself. Try to find one who is enthusiastic about your ideas and who will add to these with ideas of their own. Also fit your menu to the venue and season – fish, Mediterranean vegetables, salads and fruit would be perfect in summer, but you may want something more substantial and warming in midwinter. Most good caterers will be able to offer a choice of several different menus at a range of prices per head. They should be responsive to any specific preferences you have and may be able to mix and match menus to suit your needs.

CATERERS

✔ Do ask for references and check on the quality of food and service.

✔ Do let the caterers know *exactly* what you want – the type of food, the number of guests, budget per head, the date, time and place for the reception, theme if there is one.

✔ Do make sure you are happy with all the courses if they are offering a set menu.

✔ Do ask for a detailed quote.

✘ Don't forget to find out and tell the caterers if any of the guests have special dietary needs (not just vegetarian but also food allergies).

✘ Don't forget to tell them if numbers change.

CATERERS' QUOTES CHECKLIST

Crockery ☐

Cutlery ☐

Napkins ☐

Tablecloths ☐

Menus (as well as the food, of course!) ☐

If they are not provided by the reception venue, you should also ask the catering company to supply:

Waiting staff ☐

Staff to clear away ☐

Tables and chairs ☐

Drinks

The quantity of alcohol you need to provide will depend not only on the number of guests but also on the type of meal you are serving and how long you want the reception to last. If the venue is supplying drinks, make sure they are on a sale-or-return basis, as this can be a hefty expense. If you are bringing your own drinks, check whether there are charges for corkage.

The usual convention is to greet guests with drinks when they first arrive. Champagne, sherry and buck's fizz are all popular, but Pimms, champagne cocktails, fruit punches and other cocktails would also make suitable summer drinks, while mulled wine and schnapps could be offered at winter weddings.

Champagne is the traditional wedding drink, but there is a huge range of excellent sparkling wines which can be served throughout the reception. Alternatively, you may decide to serve wine with the meal and keep the champagne or sparkling wine for the toasts. Another option is to offer a certain number of drinks and then provide a cash bar. Also remember soft drinks for children, drivers and adults who prefer them, as well as coffee and tea.

When choosing wine, think about the food you will be serving and what will complement your menu.

Most people give guests the choice of red and white wine, or both. Your wine merchant should be able to advise you and when you are buying in bulk they will often supply on a sale-or-return basis. Most wine merchants or off-licences carry stocks of glasses to hire if you need your own and often, especially if you are also buying wine, these will effectively be free – you pay a returnable deposit and for any breakages.

Here is a rough guide to the amounts you should assume guests will drink:

As guests arrive	No. of glasses per guest	No. of glasses per bottle
Champagne or other drink	2	6–8
During the meal		
Wine	3–6	6–8
Champagne or sparkling wine for toasts	1–2	6–8
Brandy/liqueurs	1–2	
Soft drinks	0.5 to 1 litre	

If you have a theme to your wedding day, you might like to match your drinks and offer something slightly different:

- Colourful cocktails can be stylish and fun – serve in chic cocktail glasses with minimal fruit and foliage, and some subtle decoration to coordinate with your colour theme
- Chilled martinis – made with vodka or Bombay Sapphire gin
- Hot toddies for Scottish and winter weddings
- Japanese beer such as Sapporo or Kirin
- Real ale for country weddings
- Sambuca – to end a Mediterranean menu

Order of arrival and formal receiving line

The bride and groom are the first to leave the church and so arrive first at the reception, followed by parents. If the reception is informal, the bride and groom could greet guests at the door, and at a large wedding this saves time.

However, many families prefer to have a formal receiving line, in which case the traditional order is:

Bride's parents, groom's parents, bride and groom, attendants.

Reception timetable

Some couples hire a toastmaster to act as master of ceremonies and the reception venue may well provide a member of staff. If not, the best man should step into this role and should oversee the sequence of events. The toastmaster's duties can include announcing guests as they arrive, the start of the meal, toasts and speeches, the cutting of the cake and the departure of the bride and groom.

The standard timetable for a wedding would be the receiving line, the meal (if the minister is present, he should be asked to say grace), the speeches and toasts, cutting the cake (although this is sometimes done before the speeches), the departure of the bride and groom.

Seating plan

It is a good idea to work out a seating plan if you are having a sit-down meal at the reception. You can begin to draw this up as soon as you have received all the acceptances to the wedding invitations, and if you display a large plan near to the dining room guests will be able to go straight to their seats with a minimum of confusion. Name cards should be placed on the tables on the day – staff at the venue or from the caterers will do this for you usually and you should make sure they have an up-to-date copy of the seating plan. Name or place cards should be handwritten in ink.

Management at the venue will be able to advise you on the best arrangement of tables to suit the space and number of guests. Obviously no one likes to feel pushed out to the sidelines and at weddings most people prefer to be close to the top table or at least able to see.

Traditionally, at formal receptions, the closest relatives are seated nearest to the top table, followed by aunts and uncles, then friends and colleagues. As a general rule, husbands and wives are placed on the same tables but not next to one another, although they may be seated opposite. It is usual to try to alternate men and women.

Guests will spend a long time sitting at their tables and it is important to try to ensure they have fun. Seat a couple of people who know each other well on a table with others whose company you think they will find interesting. You will need to be sensitive to divorced couples and guests who do not know anyone. It's an obvious suggestion, but keep guests who really do not get along apart. Another idea is to let guests move around and mingle after the formalities are over.

If you are having an informal buffet, you can leave guests to organise their own seating arrangements. You should, however, still think about seating. Guests will not enjoy standing for long periods of time and you should make sure there are sufficient tables and chairs.

THE TOP TABLE

Even if you are having a buffet meal, there is usually a top table for the wedding party, where they are served with food. The usual order is for the bride and groom to sit together at the centre. The traditional plan is shown opposite:

Sometimes the plan is altered so the chief bridesmaid and best man sit together, or so that all the attendants are seated at the top table, and if you do need to adapt the plan, remember that couples (apart from the bride and groom) should not sit together.

If parents are divorced and remarried they should usually be seated close to their new partners. There are two suggestions opposite:

There are various reasons why these arrangements may be impossible in practice, and one quite fashionable approach to solving the problem is to have a series of circular tables with each of the key players hosting their own table.

The final decision on table and seating arrangements is yours. While being sensitive to other people, you should make sure you will enjoy yourselves, and remember, rules are made to be broken.

Traditional plan	When the groom's parents are divorced and both are remarried	When the bride's parents are divorced and both are remarried
		Bride's Stepfather
	Best Man	
Chief Bridesmaid	Groom's Stepmother	Chief Bridesmaid
Groom's Father	Groom's Father	Groom's Father
Bride's Mother	Bride's Mother	Bride's Mother
Groom	Groom	Groom
Bride	Bride	Bride
Bride's Father	Bride's Father	Bride's Father
Groom's Mother	Groom's Mother	Groom's Mother
Best Man	Groom's Stepfather	Best Man
	Chief Bridesmaid	Bride's Stepmother

THE SEATING PLAN

✓ Do try to remember who gets along and who doesn't.

✓ Do try to avoid making anyone feel they have been pushed out to the edges of the room.

✓ Do try to organise interesting groups on tables with a mix of guests who know one another and others whose company you think they will enjoy.

✓ Do opt for circular rather than rectangular tables – it makes relaxed conversation much easier.

✗ Don't sit Great-Aunt Ethel next to your most outrageous friend.

✗ If family relations are strained, with divorced parents or some family members not on speaking terms, Don't feel you have to stick rigidly to a conventional top table. Divide up the key members of the wedding party and let them host their own tables.

Children

It is entirely up to you whether or not you invite children to your wedding. But whatever you decide, you should make it clear from the beginning. At the reception, small children should always be seated with their parents. Older children or teenagers may prefer to sit at a table together.

If there are to be many small children, it might be worth organising a crèche in a nearby room, supervised by a qualified childminder. You could also

think about providing child-friendly food and an
entertainer part-way through the day.

Wedding cake

The wedding cake can be simple and stylish,
traditionally tiered or as wildly creative as you like.
It is still often seen as the decorative centrepiece of
the reception and is an important part of the
wedding ritual, following a tradition that dates back
to at least Roman times.

The bride and groom make the first cut together,
and then it is taken away to be sliced and served.
The cake-cutting usually happens immediately after
the speeches and toasts, and this marks the end of
the formal part of the reception. There are more
details about types of cakes and decorations in
Chapter 12.

Wedding favours

The tradition of giving away sweets at weddings
goes back centuries and crosses many different
cultures. They are generally associated with bringing
good luck and fertility to the couple.

Sugared almonds are the most popular – usually six
to signify health, wealth, happiness, fertility, good
luck and long life for the bride and groom. These are
prettily tied in cellophane or net, or presented in a

small beribboned box. They can be set next to place cards on the table for each guest.

Another idea, if you are having a buffet and there are no set places, would be to hand around slices of wedding cake along with the sugared almonds in ribbon-tied cellophane packages. Chocolates, tiny shaped cookies or other sweets could be offered in place of the almonds, and many companies will make up individual gift boxes, tins or packages. Foil-wrapped fortune cookies and personalised miniature bottles of liqueurs or other spirits are also available.

Single-use cameras

A recent wedding trend has been to place throw-away cameras on tables or dotted around for guests to use. These are inexpensive and can provide you with an informal, fun record of your day. Ask guests to return them at the end of the reception for you to process.

Music and entertainment

When you are attempting to create an atmosphere, a key element is music. A quartet or soloist is especially effective at the reception, particularly when guests are arriving and during the meal. At outdoor summer weddings, small jazz groups, singers and steel bands can add a lively fun feel to the day. There are a number of music companies that will provide everything from harpists to themed wedding music, Elvis-lookalikes and barbershop quartets. You may also want to think about other entertainers – magicians, jugglers, even a clown or puppets if there are going to be many children.

If your reception is continuing into the evening, you will probably want to add to the party atmosphere by booking a DJ or a live band. It is a wedding convention that the bride and groom dance the first dance together and it is worth thinking about what you want this to be. Often couples choose a romantic song – Nat King Cole's 'Unforgettable' and 'Love is All Around' are popular – but it could be anything that is special to you as a couple, or a song that just makes you happy and want to dance. It doesn't have to sound particularly appropriate to anyone else.

To economise, you could think about recorded music. It might be worth making your own tapes and asking a friend to oversee the playing for you. Remember to include some more gentle music to play during the meal and while guests are chatting. You could think about hiring or borrowing suitable equipment to use for the day.

You can find musical agencies, entertainers and DJs in *Yellow Pages*, the listings in bride and other magazines, and on wedding websites.

RECEPTION ENTERTAINMENT

✓ Do ask friends for recommendations.

✓ Do listen to a recording, watch a video of them performing or go along to another gig before you book anyone.

✓ Do discuss the types of music you want before the reception.

✓ Do find out what is included in the quote – travel fees, VAT and specialist equipment can all be extras.

✓ Do book as far ahead as possible.

Doves

Victoria Beckham is just one celebrity bride who released doves at her wedding, and while most brides don't free a whole flock, there is a growing trend for releasing a pair of white doves. Just like homing pigeons, doves find their own way home, and the cost of hiring them depends on distance and the number of birds.

DOVES

The White Dove Company: 020 8508 1414

Animal Actors: 020 8654 0450

Fireworks

Round off your celebration with a bang. There's always something exciting about fireworks and several companies offer a specialist wedding service.

You can choose from operator-fired displays or DIY packs, but always check with your reception venue first.

FIREWORKS

Celebration Displays: 0161 723 4422, or
- **www.celebrationdisplays.co.uk**

Brilliant Fireworks: 0800 458 3355, or
- **www.brilliantfireworks.co.uk**

9 WEDDING DRESSES, SUITS & RINGS

Weddings are, of course, about much more than clothes, but what you choose to wear does help to set the whole tone for your wedding day.

Most people's accounts of a wedding include a detailed description of the bride's dress, what her mother wore and the choice of bridesmaids' dresses. Nowadays, the groom does not escape attention either, and increasingly the suits and styles chosen by the groom, best man and other male attendants attract just as much notice as the outfits worn by the bridal party.

For most brides, popping out to the shops a few days before the wedding to sort out what you want to wear will simply not be an option. You aren't going to be able to find your perfect dress hanging on a rack waiting for you. If you are having a dress specially made or altered or customised, time must be allowed.

The same goes for the groom. While hiring a wedding suit is now quite the norm, to get exactly what you want in the right size and with matching outfits for the rest of the gents in the bridal party means booking your dress hire well in advance.

THE BRIDE'S DRESS

Your wedding day is the one occasion when you are going to be the centre of attention. Every bride wants to look her best and most brides begin thinking about a wedding dress very soon after the engagement. You will never get the chance to dress up like this again, so make the most of it. Choosing should be fun. Give yourself plenty of time and don't rush into buying.

There are all kinds of superstitions surrounding the bride's dress and even modern brides take note of some, in particular that it is bad luck for the groom to see the wedding dress before the ceremony.

According to folklore, the complete wedding outfit must not be worn before the day and the veil should not be tried on at the same time as the dress. Some brides would put their veil on for the first time only as they left for their wedding. Most brides today prefer to make sure that dress and veil look right together beforehand.

It was also said that the bride should not make her dress herself. Some also believed that the dress should not even be finished until the day and purposely left a few stitches to be completed on the wedding morning.

The colour of the wedding dress is also important. Everyone knows that a white dress is a symbol of virginity or purity, but before white dresses were first worn in Elizabethan times, brides simply wore their best dress, although it was thought wise to avoid certain colours. Green was particularly unlucky as it was the fairies' colour and the wearer might fall under the spell of the little people. The phrase 'a green gown' was used to refer to a 'loose' woman whose dress was green from grass stains, from rolling in meadows. The colours yellow, purple and orange were also to be avoided for wedding dresses.

Initial ideas

When choosing a dress, you could begin by looking through bride magazines. They will quickly give you an idea of the styles that are around and any trends. Think about the type of ceremony you are planning and what would be appropriate. Or perhaps you have always had a dream image of the dress you want. Cut out pictures of anything you especially like and keep them in your wedding file. An early 'just looking' trip is a good idea, and take your mother or best friend with you when you start trying on dresses.

- Long dresses, often in white or off-white, are most appropriate for church or traditional weddings.
- There are no rules for civil weddings – you could choose a long dress, but a stylish suit would not be out of place.

- If your wedding is in summer or late spring, light fabrics look best and would be the most comfortable to wear.
- If you are marrying in winter or autumn, choose heavier material and think about a matching jacket or cloak.

Where to buy

An average wedding dress costs around £700, though it is possible to spend far less, while a bespoke designer dress will cost considerably more.

Bespoke is the equivalent of couture, with everything handmade throughout the whole process. This is different from 'made to measure' or 'made to order', where existing patterns are used.

Specialist wedding shops and department stores

These carry a wide variety of styles at a range of prices and you can often buy all the accessories from the same place. Some designers are now designing for high street stores – Jasper Conran, for instance, at Debenhams. It is sensible to telephone first as you may need an appointment if you want to try something on. Most stores will be able to fit the dress and make any essential alterations, but this can take up to eight weeks before the dress is ready.

Bride magazines carry advertisements for retailers, designers and couture suppliers, and wedding websites are another good source of addresses.

THE WEDDING DRESS

- ✔ Do start looking early.
- ✔ Do check the sales – there are sometimes great bargains to be found.

Dressmakers

A one-off designer dress would be very costly but would ensure your dress was unique. Another less expensive option would be to find a style you like and ask a dressmaker to make it for you. Butterick and Vogue patterns include some from design houses such as Givenchy and Donna Karan.

DRESSMAKING

- ✔ Do find an experienced dressmaker or one who is highly recommended. If you are very confident or skilled, you could make the dress yourself but …
- ✔ Do remember that you will be very busy in the run-up to your wedding.
- ✔ Do try making up the dress in a cheap fabric first, if you decide to make it yourself.
- ✔ Do ask a friend or relative who is also a dressmaker to help you with the final fitting, as it is almost impossible to achieve a perfect fit alone.
- ✔ Do allow yourself plenty of time.

Hiring and second-hand dresses

If you are not planning to keep your dress after the wedding, hiring could be a good option. It may mean that you can wear a stunning dress without paying a fortune. You will still need to allow plenty of time and should book a dress at least twelve weeks before the wedding day.

DRESS HIRE

✓ Do ask for a written agreement that the dress you have chosen will be available on the right date and that it will have been returned by the previous wearer and cleaned.

✓ Do make sure that the dress will be available beforehand to check accessories.

✓ Do arrange for your chief bridesmaid to return the dress after the ceremony.

Another option is a second-hand dress agency. It may be possible to find a designer dress (worn once) at a very reasonable price. The advantage of buying over hiring is that the dress can be altered to your own specifications and can be adapted specially for you.

• **www.webwedding.co.uk** has a wedding dress swapshop.

Borrowing

You may be surprised. Your dream dress could be lying carefully stored at your parents' home. Or perhaps a recently married friend has a dress you could borrow.

Dress style

By looking through magazines and in bridal departments, you will soon have an idea of current style trends, or you may favour a classic design. Historically, queens and royal brides wore silver gowns. Queen Victoria broke with tradition to wear white and this has been the favoured colour ever since. White is still popular for wedding dresses, but silver and pale gold have also regained popularity.

You will already have an idea of the colours and styles that suit you best but it is always worth trying something different. Some dresses that appear quite ordinary on the hanger can look sensational on.

DRESS TIPS

✓ Do consider what the back of your dress looks like and think about the details, because this is the view that most people will see during the ceremony.

✓ Do pay attention to detail. Well-chosen accessories can transform the look of the simplest dress and make your outfit outstanding.

STYLE TIPS

- Pure white can be difficult to wear, particularly for pale skins – ivory or off-white may be more flattering.
- A simple fitted bodice or corset, with or without straps, can be very flattering. It makes the most of the smaller bust and, when worn with a full or A-line skirt, can also work well on fuller figures.
- A fitted, bias-cut dress or column shape suits tall slim figures and well-proportioned women as the fabric follows the curves of the body.
- If you have broader hips and legs, choose a fitted top falling into a flat A-line skirt.
- Empire-line dresses, where the bodice is fitted to just below the bust and the skirt is quite narrow, are flattering for petite women and also help to camouflage thick waistlines.
- If you want to wear a strapless dress but want something less revealing (or warmer) for the ceremony, add a sheer or lace bolero with sleeves.

Preserving your wedding dress

Whether you bought your wedding dress or had it made exclusively for you, it is special and many brides want to preserve their dresses as a memento of their wedding day.

Brides used to rely on careful wrapping and packing their dress between layers of tissue paper, but the most effective method of preserving a dress now is to have it professionally vacuum-packed. The process takes about two weeks. It costs £60 to have the dress vacuum-packed and boxed, and £100-£300 for cleaning. Contact: Elias, tel: 020 7584 1246.

VEILS AND ACCESSORIES

Veils

Bridal veils may be a throwback to the times when eager grooms would simply fling a blanket over the bride's head and carry her off. Alternatively, they might date from Roman times, when a veil was worn to guard against evil spirits.

Wedding veils gained popularity in Britain in the 19th century and originally covered the bride's face as she entered the church. They have become popular again as they can be very flattering. They look romantic and complete the image. There are now many styles to choose from and some are subtly trimmed – with tiny crystals to catch the light, delicate flower petals, embroidery and even feathers. Newer shapes include rectangular, square and pointed veils.

VEIL TIPS

- Silk tulle or net drapes softly and is very light.
- Lace looks traditional. Antique lace veils can still be found and are very soft, although they often need a tiara to hold them in place as they can be heavy.
- Synthetic net can give a fuller shape, but it is often slippery and hard to hold in place.
- If you are wearing a period wedding dress, it is best to choose a veil dating from the same era.

- Veils can be worn to any length and can have more than one layer. They can frame the face, be piled high over a headdress or bunched and ruched at the back of the head.
- Wear your wedding dress when choosing a veil to help you find the perfect style.

VEIL LENGTHS
- Fingertip – ends at the point where your fingertips skim your dress
- Mantilla (from the Spanish) – a short lace-trimmed veil that frames your face
- Church – a full-length veil
- Cathedral – longer even than your dress and train, if you have one.

Headdresses

Headdresses can serve a practical purpose by holding your veil in place, but they can also complete your look – and how many other occasions allow you to wear one?

Choose from fresh or silk flowers, decorative combs, circlets, Alice bands, tiaras and crowns using coloured crystals, gems, gilt, pearls, feathers and enamel. You will find flowers, birds, butterflies and any number of designs to complement your veil, dress, bouquet or even the colour of your eyes.

Look in specialist bridal shops and check bride magazines for features and advertisements.

Hair

Having found the right dress, the veil and the headdress, now is the time to decide on your hairstyle.

HAIR

✓ Do make sure your hair is in good condition.
✓ Do have it cut and recoloured if necessary two to three weeks before the wedding to allow it to settle down.

When choosing a style for the day, there are a number of points to consider.

HAIR TIPS

- Consider your dress and what hairstyle would best complement it
- Try out different styles with your headdress and veil
- Ensure the style looks good from every angle, including the back, which is what guests will be looking at during the ceremony
- Think about how it will look in photographs
- Remember that your hair needs to look good all day – you don't want to have to keep repairing or repinning your style
- Try out any new style with your hairstylist before the wedding
- You don't have to change your hair – you may feel happiest with a perfected version of your normal style

For more information on wedding hair, see Chapter 15.

Lingerie

Underwear should be bought after you have chosen your dress. Wedding lingerie, in particular, should fit well, look beautiful and make you feel sexy. Your wedding day is the time to splash out on something special.

Bride magazines and wedding websites all carry advertisements for stockists.

You could also try La Perla, Agent Provocateur, and Rigby and Peller.

Shoes

Shoes, like all accessories, should not be bought until you know what style and colour dress you will be wearing. It is a good idea to start looking as soon as you have chosen the dress, though, because you will need to know the height of the heels before you can finalise the length of the dress.

When you order your dress, ask for a swatch of the material to take with you when looking for shoes to match colour and texture. There is a wider range of shoes for weddings than ever before, both from specialist shops and retailers like Emma Hope and LK Bennett. It is not difficult to find both plain and embroidered silk shoes in white and a rainbow of other colours, sandals and slingbacks with pearls, ribbons, flowers and diamanté, and every height of heel.

If you have searched everywhere and still can't find the perfect colour match, it is possible to have shoes professionally dyed. This can be particularly useful for bridesmaids' shoes. Some retailers offer this service themselves and you should allow about three weeks. The cost is around £40 for shoes and £30 for bags.

SHOES

- ✔ Do remember the time of year. Strappy sandals could leave you freezing and wet in the winter months.
- ✔ Do make sure shoes are comfortable. You will be wearing them for several hours.
- ✔ Do wear shoes before the day to break them in.
- ✗ Don't mark them or damage them before the day. They should be comfy, but they shouldn't look old.

STOCKISTS

Anello & Davide: 020 7225 2468

Emma Hope: 020 7259 9566

LK Bennett: 020 7491 3005

Make-up and manicures

It is worth making an appointment to see a professional make-up consultant before your wedding. They will be able to give you tips on how to apply make-up and what best suits you – as well as offering advice on make-up for photographs and how to define your features. You probably don't want a dramatic new look – just a perfected version of your natural style.

Book an appointment with your best friend or chief bridesmaid. Make a day of it and have fun.

Department-store beauty counters are a good start. Fees charged are often redeemable against any products bought and you may even find that wedding make-overs are free. Ask for a chart of all the products used and quiz the consultant for professional tips.

MAKE-UP

✓ Do make natural-coloured lips look fuller by adding a touch of paler colour in the middle.

✓ Do ask your chief bridesmaid or mother to carry a mini make-up case of essentials for you on the day.

✓ Do apply foundation with a damp sponge and finish with translucent powder.

✔ Do think about the mascara and eyeliner you wear – are you likely to cry? If so, it might be wise to pick waterproof brands.

✘ Don't try anything new on the morning of your wedding – always experiment beforehand and ask a good friend for an honest opinion.

✘ Don't wear lipstick that clashes with your bridesmaids'.

✘ Don't use very pale make-up and lipstick – it does not look great in photos.

Dark shades of lipstick, especially red, look even darker in black-and-white photos. Pink and brown shades of lipstick make teeth look whiter.

It is worth considering a visit to a beauty salon before the wedding to have eyebrows plucked, eyelashes tinted and legs waxed. All of these should be done at least four days before the wedding and slightly longer if you have very sensitive skin.

The bride's hands are on display at a wedding. They feature in many wedding photos from signing the register to cutting the cake, and everyone will want to take a look at the ring. A professional manicure at your favourite salon the day before the wedding is one way to ensure you're looking good. You could treat yourself to a pedicure at the same time.

Something old, something new

*Something old, something new, something borrowed,
something blue.*

This tradition dates back to Saxon times. 'Something
old' stresses the bride's link with her past and her
own family, and she will sometimes wear a piece of
her grandmother's jewellery. 'Something new'
represents the future, bringing success and wealth
in her new life, and is often the wedding dress.
'Something borrowed' links the bride to the present
and brings good luck. It should also remind her that
old friends and family are still there to support her.
Traditionally, the borrowed item should have been
worn at another, happy wedding and can be
anything, although it is usually a garter or borrowed
jewellery. 'Something blue' dates from Saxon times
when blue represented purity, and many brides
nowadays choose to wear a blue garter.

Going-away outfit

There are no rules for what you should choose,
though most brides opt for something quite stylish.
If you are going away on honeymoon immediately
after the reception, you should find something
suitable for travelling and bear in mind the
temperature of your destination. One solution may
be to find something with a jacket that you can take

off later. You could also take along extra layers to add if you are cold while travelling or sitting on a plane.

Useful websites to check for wedding style:
- **www.weddings.co.uk**
- **www.confetti.co.uk**
- **www.hitched.co.uk**
- **www.all-about-weddings.co.uk**

OTHER DRESSES

The bridesmaids' dresses

When searching for bridesmaids' dresses, it is worth visiting many of the same stockists you tried for wedding dresses. Obviously the styles you choose will depend on the type of dress you are wearing and the look you are hoping to achieve.

You may have a very definite idea of the colour you want, particularly if you have an overall colour theme. Whether you are having only adult bridesmaids, or a mixture of small children and adults, not all the dresses need to be the same, and it is often better if dresses are chosen to flatter bridesmaids' individual figures. It is a good idea to have some feature which gives a sense of uniformity, but it should be possible to draw the group together with accessories – for instance, the same posies, bags, jewellery, shoes or sashes.

If you are on a budget, it is worth checking high street stores for pretty dresses. With hair ornaments, bouquets, shoes and other accessories you can personalise the outfits so no one would guess where they came from.

BRIDESMAID'S DRESSES

✓ Do have a meeting with bridesmaids to discuss ideas and the overall look.

✓ Do make it clear whether you are happy for the bridesmaids to choose their own outfits or if you want to oversee the selection.

✓ Do make it clear whether or not you are paying for the dresses – if you are, you should definitely have the final say.

✓ Don't force your bridesmaids to wear something you would not wear yourself.

The bride's mother

As the bride's mother you are one of the most important members of the wedding party after the bride, and what you wear will receive a lot of attention. It is no longer necessary to go for a classic suit and fashion plays a big part in the choice of outfit. The best option is to pick something that develops your normal style and suits your particular colouring and figure.

As with any outfit, accessories – shoes, bags, scarves, jewellery – are always important and can really complete the outfit. Hats are not essential, but if you enjoy wearing them there are more styles and shades now than ever to choose from.

BRIDE'S MOTHER'S OUTFIT

✔ Do let the groom's mother know what you are wearing.
It could save the embarrassment of matching too well
or clashing horribly.

THE GROOM'S OUTFIT

On average, British grooms spend less than half the amount spent by the bride on a wedding outfit. It is, however, just as important for the groom to look good on the day and over the past few years there has been an increasing focus on men's fashion.

The choice of wedding attire is huge and modern grooms can choose from morning suits, frock coats, Nehru jackets, tuxedos, smart lounge suits and even kilts, in a range of colours and styles.

It is best to discuss possible styles with the bride. Without knowing exactly what the bride and bridesmaids will be wearing, it may still be possible to coordinate colours by choosing a tie, cummerbund or waistcoat, for instance, to match dresses or flowers.

Hiring

More than 50 per cent of grooms hire their wedding outfits. If you are planning to do this, it is advisable to have two fittings, one a few months and one two to three weeks before the wedding. It is also worth remembering that hire companies often have plenty of average-size suits but may not be as well stocked with other sizes. The average cost is roughly £50.

SUIT HIRE

Moss Bros: 020 7447 7200 (175 stores nationwide), or
• www.mossbros.co.uk

Youngs Hire at Suits You: 020 8327 3005 (30 stores nationwide)

Virgin Brides: 0161 829 8900, or
• www.virginbrides.co.uk

Pronuptia Men's Formal Wear:
• www.pronuptia.co.uk

Lords Formal Wear: 020 7538 0333, or
• www.lords-formal-wear.com

London Menswear: 020 7701 4499, or
• www.londonbrideandgroom.co.uk

Keogh & Savage: 0141 778 2308 (includes highland wear, based in Glasgow)

Morning suits are traditionally worn for church weddings and consist of a black tailcoat with grey or black striped trousers, or sometimes a grey tailcoat and grey trousers. It is usual to wear a waistcoat with the suit.

Black tie Dinner jackets, or tuxedos, and black ties (which in practice can be almost any colour) have long been worn in the United States and Europe for weddings, and they are now gaining popularity in this country, especially for late afternoon or evening ceremonies and register offices. Let guests know by printing 'Black tie' at the bottom right-hand corner of your invitations.

Waistcoats can add a personal touch to a hired suit. Traditionally, buff or grey waistcoats were worn with morning suits, but this is no longer the rule and coloured and embroidered waistcoats are an excellent way to coordinate with the bride and bridesmaids and express your own style.

WEDDING WAISTCOATS

Favourbrook: 020 7491 2337, or

• **www.favourbrook.com**

Fantasy Waistcoats: 0121 353 2848

Bespoke suits

These are made by hand and involve a number of fittings to cut the suit exactly to your specifications. The suit is not made from a pattern and is cut and fitted on the individual by a tailor and fitter. The fit and specifications are reassessed by the tailor at every stage. This is the most expensive way to buy a suit, but if you want personal service and a really special suit this is what to go for.

Made to measure

Made-to-measure suits are chosen from a range of styles and fabrics and tailored to you. They are cheaper than bespoke suits because they are made from existing patterns, factory-cut and there is usually only one fitting. Alterations can be made, free of charge, when the suit is ready if you have lost or gained weight.

Groom's buttonhole

Traditionally, this comes from the bride's bouquet.

Shirts

The style and colour chosen are a matter of personal preference but you should avoid shirts with pockets as these are too casual for a wedding or formal occasion.

Collars made from two pieces of fabric sit better and also mean you can use collar stiffeners. A vertical cut at the back, called a split yoke, also gives the collar a better fit. Conventionally, a couple of centimetres of shirt cuff should be visible below the sleeves of your jacket and carefully chosen cufflinks add detail.

GROOM'S WEDDING OUTFIT

✓ Do start looking early, even if you are planning to hire.
✓ Do look at bride magazines for ideas.
✓ Do ask to be measured before trying anything on.
✓ Do take someone with you for advice when choosing your outfit.
✓ Do consult the bride before making your final choice.
✓ Do coordinate with the best man and ushers.
✓ Don't clash with the bride.

✗ Don't choose anything too tight-fitting. It will look terrible in the photographs and be uncomfortable on the day.

✗ Don't wear new shoes for the first time to your wedding. Break them in by wearing them at home.

Useful websites for groom's wedding attire:

- www.marcwallace.co.uk
- www.mossbros.co.uk
- www.richardjames.co.uk
- www.jonesbootmaker.com
- www.lordsformalwear.com
- www.favourbrook.com
- www.weddings.co.uk
- www.confetti.co.uk

WEDDING RINGS

Rings are a symbol of married life. A ring has no beginning and no end and was traditionally thought to symbolise unity for lovers. The wedding ring is symbolic of the pledge made by the groom that he will honour his part of the marriage contract. An exchange of rings is a standard part of most wedding ceremonies and in the Church of England it is compulsory for the bride to be given a ring.

The finger upon which you wore a ring was once considered very significant. If you were unwilling to marry, a ring was worn on the little finger of the left hand, while a ring on the index finger suggested you were searching for a partner.

Wedding and engagement rings are traditionally worn on the third finger of the left hand. Any other finger is considered unlucky. This possibly dates from the time of the Egyptians and the early Greeks, who wrongly believed that an artery ran directly from this finger to the heart. The symbol of the unbroken circle of the ring has certainly been a powerful one from ancient times, symbolising unity for lovers.

Wedding rings were often made from gold which was believed to have magical powers and until quite recently wedding rings were rubbed on warts and styes to charm them away. Taking off your wedding ring or lending it to someone was thought to be a bad idea because if it was lost your marriage could suffer the same fate. Second-hand rings were also thought to bring bad luck.

Styles

The classic wedding ring is a plain gold band, but recently platinum and more decorative rings have come to account for about 40 per cent of the market. As more couples live together before marriage, many opt for a combined wedding and engagement ring, which tends to mean the wedding band will include a gemstone. Many rings are also now made from more than one metal or have several bands twisted together.

Scottish gold rings

The tradition of exchanging rings made from Scottish gold goes back to the 1540s. It is still possible to buy Scottish gold rings with intricate Celtic knotwork designs.

For more information, try:
• **www.siliconglen.com**

Where to buy

When looking for ideas, it is worth visiting design fairs and also areas where jewellers and jewellery workshops are concentrated. This should give you an idea of different styles and also a comparison of prices at a range of different outlets.

JEWELLERS

The Goldsmiths' Company: 020 7606 7010

The Hockley district of Birmingham

Hatton Garden in London

National Association of Goldsmiths: 020 7613 4445

For the biggest internet jewellery range, try

• **www.jewellers.net**

Jewellery designers

There are many wonderful jewellery designers whom you can commission to make a ring for you. You may have your own design in mind, but it is usually better to discuss ideas with a professional who will be able to advise you about what will work best. Some retailers will also make up designs.

Contact the British Jewellers' Association, tel: 0121 237 1110, for the names of designers endorsed by the association.

Jewellers

If you are buying from a shop, choose a reputable jewellers. Ask for recommendations and contact the National Association of Goldsmiths, tel: 020 7613 4445, for a list of members in your area. Shop around. Compare quality and prices.

Choosing a ring

If you already have an engagement ring, you will obviously want your wedding ring to match and the two rings should complement each other when worn together. Usually, the engagement and wedding rings are made of the same metal. It is worth remembering that platinum is harder than gold and can wear gold away if worn next to a gold ring for a long time.

Size All jewellers will measure your finger. A ring should slip easily over the knuckle. You should be able to fit a toothpick between your finger and the ring. This allows room for your finger to swell when it's hot, but ensures that the ring won't fall off if your finger shrinks in the cold.

Gold Pure gold is a soft metal and is mixed with other metals in an alloy to make it stronger. The amount of gold is measured in carats: 24 carat is the purest normally available but also the softest; 9 carat is hardest and cheapest; 18 carat gold is a good compromise between purity and durability. Most diamonds are set in 18 carat gold. The colour ranges from white through yellow to rosy pink.

Platinum Platinum is very hard and there is no need to mix it with other metals for strength. It is silver in colour and similar to white gold, but it is more expensive.

Silver Silver is cheaper than either gold or platinum but it is a soft metal and will wear away and scratch over time.

A ring for the groom

About 75 per cent of married men wear wedding rings. These are often plain bands, slightly wider than bride's rings, but there's no reason why the groom's ring design should not mirror the bride's.

10 WEDDING PHOTOGRAPHS & VIDEOS

Everybody must have heard the complaint, 'I hate having my photo taken. I always look dreadful.' No one wants to feel that way about their wedding photographs, which should be a permanent, happy reminder of the day. It is important to choose the right photographer – one who can demonstrate technical skills as well as creativity and whose general style is in line with your ideas.

Before you contact a photographer, discuss with your partner the sorts of photos you like and look at friends' wedding pictures.

Choosing a photographer

Recommendation from someone whose wedding photos you have seen and admired is probably the best way to find a photographer. Otherwise, contact one of the professional bodies, such as the Master Photographers' Association, the Guild of Wedding Photographers or the British Institute of Professional Photographers, who will all be able to recommend approved photographers in your area. These associations will also be able to arbitrate should anything go wrong. Bride magazines, bridal fairs, wedding websites and *Yellow Pages* are other good sources to try. Many photographers also have their own website which you could look up.

WHEN LOOKING AT A PORTFOLIO

✓ Is there a good mix of different types of shots?
✓ Do couples look relaxed and happy?
✓ Is the photo well composed? Does it focus on its subject?
✓ Do the photographs make the most of the setting?
✓ Do they give a flavour of the day's character?
✓ Can the photographer offer a digital service to download your photos onto a computer?

It is always a good idea to visit a few photographers and view their specimen albums. Try to see all the shots of one wedding rather than the best from a selection of different weddings and check that the photos are recent. Larger companies sometimes pass on commissions to freelance photographers, so you should make sure you are talking to the person who will actually be taking your photos.

PHOTOGRAPHY ASSOCIATIONS

British Institute of Professional Photography: 01920 464011, or

● www.bipp.com.

Guild of Wedding Photographers: 01225 760088, or
- **www.gwp-uk.co.uk**.
Master Photographers' Association: 01325 356555, or
- **www.mpauk.com** or **www.mpawedding.co.uk**.
Society of Wedding and Portrait Photographers: 01745 356935
Kodak PhotoNet online:
- **www.kodak.co.uk**.
- **www.qm4.com**

Talk to friends. If they have used the same photographer, ask them about their experiences. Did the photographer keep everyone standing around? Was he or she professional in approach? Did he or she deliver what was promised?

THE PHOTOGRAPHER

- ✓ Do question the photographer about how certain shots were achieved – some apparently natural pictures require a great deal of skill.
- ✓ Do ask to see qualifications and check that the photographer is a member of a professional association.
- ✓ Do make sure the photographer has indemnity insurance.
- ✓ Do make sure the photographer can recreate any special effects you are keen on.

✔ Do you like the photographer? It is important to feel relaxed and this will have a big impact on the final quality of the shots and how happy you look in them. The best photographers can make you and your guests forget they are being photographed.

✔ Don't settle for a photographer who won't listen to your ideas.

✔ Don't forget to book well ahead of your wedding date. Good wedding photographers are in demand.

Costs

Fees charged vary enormously. A basic package can start from a little under £200, but the average spent by couples is more like £500. It's a truism, but you do tend to get what you pay for. It is always worth shopping around and asking more than one photographer for a quote. That way, you should have an idea of what is a reasonable price for what you want.

When quoted a price, always get it in writing and check exactly what is included – development, travel costs and VAT should all be part of the package.

The price will depend upon:

• the amount of time a photographer is spending at your wedding
• the total number of shots to be taken

- the number of pictures to be selected for the final album (the standard number is 20)
- the quality of the photograph album
- types of photograph

When you have chosen a photographer, you should have a pre-wedding meeting to discuss exactly what you want. Many professional photographers will already be familiar with local wedding and reception venues. If not, ask them to visit to check on things like lighting and space, and work out a contingency plan for bad weather.

Some photographers will offer to take a few trial photographs of you before the wedding to find out what works best for you. If parents are paying, invite them along to meet the photographer and view past work. Sometimes parents have a fixed view on style and favour traditional pictures when you particularly want an informal reportage style. Do be prepared to compromise – ask the photographer to take pictures in both styles.

Styles of photograph

Wedding photography is now much more creative and individual than in the past. You should let your photographer know which styles you prefer and make sure such pictures are in his or her normal repertoire.

PHOTOGRAPHER CHECKLIST

Discuss the types of shots you would like and
how many. ☐

Tell the photographer about any awkward
family situations. ☐

Let him or her know the names of family and friends
you particularly want photographed (perhaps ask
one of the ushers to help out and organise groups). ☐

Let the photographer know the number of guests,
how long the ceremony is and any restrictions on
photography. ☐

Make sure the photographer has all the correct
addresses for venues and the correct times. ☐

Classic romantic These are often popular with older
relatives and don't have to be dull. There should be a
balance of formal and informal or candid shots, with
subjects looking happy and relaxed.

Reportage This style is becoming increasingly
popular and the naturalness belies the skill needed
to do it well. The approach avoids obvious poses and
catches the more impromptu moments of the day.
Weddings are spontaneous and, however well
planned, there are usually a few surprises – hopefully
all captured on camera, along with casually romantic
shots of the bride and groom.

Storybook This approach tries to provide a record of the whole event, beginning with the morning preparations. It is very like reportage in avoiding obvious poses. In addition, if the photographer is known to the minister or registrar, discreet photos taken during the ceremony are usually allowed. You can still have the more standard group shots, as well as some fun, informal shots, at the reception later, when everyone is more relaxed.

Black and white These photographs can look very stylish and effective. Of course, you won't be able to see the colour of the flowers or the bridesmaids' dresses and it is probably worth having colour pictures taken as well.

Sepia prints are another variation. They can look softer than black and white and the muted tones are often very flattering.

Hand-tinting is a further variation and, if done sparingly and by an experienced photographer, this can be effective.

DIGITAL CAMERAS

Digital cameras record images in the way that a computer memorises a word-processing document. The images can then be downloaded on to a computer and transferred to a floppy disk or CD. You can then make your own colour printouts and email them to friends and family. It is also possible to make your own wedding website with the pictures and manipulate the images yourself. Software is readily available to allow colour correcting and even to change pictures from colour to black and white.

DIGITAL IMAGING
Photographs can be digitally enhanced to improve quality and even to change backgrounds. This process can also be used to remove any blemishes. Check whether your photographer can offer this service.

THROWAWAY CAMERAS
A trend that has really taken off is to place disposable cameras on tables at the reception. Guests can then take photos of your wedding from their own perspective. They can be collected at the end of the reception and developed to give an alternative view of the day.

Traditional wedding shots
Before the wedding, agree a list of essential shots which must be taken. If your budget allows, try to include a mix of classic, formal or posed photographs, as well as candid, more natural ones and romantic, stylish shots; and opt for colour and black and white. On the day, it may be a good idea to ask the best man to make sure that no one is left out.

POSSIBLE SHOTS BEFORE THE CEREMONY

Close-up of the bride ❑

Bridesmaids helping the bride ❑

Bride putting on veil ❑

Bride with mother ❑

Bride with father ❑

Bride with parents ❑

Mother and father ❑

Bride with family ❑

Bride with sister(s) ❑

Bride with chief bridesmaid ❑

Bride and father getting into wedding car ❑

Mother and bridesmaids leaving ❑

POSSIBLE SHOTS ARRIVING AT THE CEREMONY

Groom ❑

Groom, best man and ushers ❑

Groom and best man ❑

Groom and his parents ❑

Groom and his father ❑

Guests arriving ❑

Ushers helping guests ❑

Bride's mother and bridesmaids ❏

Bride's mother ❏

Arrival of the bride ❏

Bride and father ❏

Bride, bridesmaids and father ❏

Bride's father and vicar ❏

Bride and parents ❏

Bridesmaids individually and as a group ❏

The church exterior/interior
with guests, flowers, etc. ❏

POSSIBLE SHOTS DURING THE CEREMONY

*Always check beforehand whether or not photography
is allowed.*

Exchange of vows ❏

Exchange of rings ❏

General view of the ceremony ❏

Bride and father walking down the aisle ❏

Organist ❏

Choir ❏

Bride and groom signing the register ❏

Group shot of bridal party signing the register ❏

Bride signing the register ❏

Bride and groom and witnesses ❏

Bride, groom and parents ❏

Bridal party leaving the church ❏

Bride and groom leaving the church ❏

Bridesmaids walking down the aisle ❏

Bride and groom with the vicar and
certificate of marriage ❏

Bride and groom walking down the aisle
(recessional) ❏

Groom and best man at the altar (if this is
permitted) ❏

POSSIBLE SHOTS OUTSIDE THE CHURCH

Bride with mothers ❏

Bride with fathers ❏

Groom with mothers ❏

Groom with fathers ❏

Bride ❏

Groom ❏

Bride and bridesmaids ❏

Groom and best man ❏

Groom and bridesmaids ❏

Groom and bridesmaids ❏

Bride, groom and best man ❏

Bride and chief bridesmaid ❏

Bride, best man and ushers ❏

Bride and groom with fathers ❏

Bride and groom at the church door ❏

Bride, groom, best man and bridesmaids ❏

Bride, groom, best man and ushers ❏

Bride, groom and bride's parents ❏

Bride, groom and groom's parents ❏

Bride, groom and both sets of parents ❏

Bride and groom with mothers ❏

Bride and groom with both families ❏

Bride and groom with wedding party ❏

Bride and groom with wedding party and guests ❏

Bride and groom with special friends ❏

Bride and groom being showered with confetti
(if permitted) ❏

Bride and groom getting into wedding car or
vehicle ❏

Bride and groom leaving for the reception ❏

POSSIBLE SHOTS AT THE RECEPTION

Bride and groom arriving ❑

Parents arriving ❑

Bride and groom going inside ❑

The receiving line ❑

Panorama of the venue ❑

Bridesmaids ❑

Bridesmaids and best man ❑

Tables ❑

Flowers and decorations ❑

Wedding cake ❑

Speeches ❑

Toasts ❑

Musicians ❑

Bride, groom and guests ❑

Bride, groom and attendants ❑

Dining room or marquee ❑

Bride and groom cutting cake ❑

Bride and groom in the grounds ❑

Guests – including special friends ❑

Bride outside – full-length and close-up ❑

Groom outside – full-length and close-up ❑

Bride and groom's first dance ❑

Bride and father dancing ❑

Bride and groom's father dancing ☐

Groom and mother dancing ☐

Groom and bride's mother dancing ☐

Throwing and catching bouquet ☐

Bride and groom getting into car ☐

Car leaving – shot of rear of car as it drives away ☐

If the ceremony venue is not particularly pretty, the photographer may suggest another location for some of those shots – a nearby park or flower garden, for instance, or reserve more shots for the reception, especially if it is a particularly stunning setting.

Posting photos on the net

Fotango is Europe's first online, high-quality photo processing service. It will develop your wedding photos and allows you to set up your own wedding album online. Friends and relations can view your wedding photos anywhere in the world and also order prints. The service itself is free, you just pay for any photographs you order. Go to:

• **www.fotango.com**

Copyright

The copyright of your wedding photos remains with the photographer and he or she will usually keep the negatives, which means you will always have to go back to the photographer for extra prints. Copyright law dictates that negatives should be stored for 50 years and it is wise to check with the photographer what will happen to yours.

Sometimes photographers will include the negatives as part of the deal, so you can have extra prints made up yourself.

Viewing your photographs

Usually the photographs will be ready for you to see when you return from the honeymoon. Don't forget that when you first see the prints they are preview shots, and they can be improved by cropping and framing.

Photographers tend to allow about a month for ordering prints and it should take about six weeks for them to arrive.

When things go wrong

Unfortunately, disasters do happen, however careful you have been in your choice of photographer.

You must ensure that your photographer has professional indemnity insurance, which should provide cover for accidental damage or injury to people or property, failure to produce work and for spoiled or lost photographs. This means that the insurance company will pay for the photographs to be retaken, although obviously this will not be the same as having them done on your wedding day. You should also check your own wedding insurance policy if you have one. Some will pay up to £2,000 compensation for ruined photos.

If there is a dispute and the photographer is a member of one of the professional associations, the association should help out and act as a mediator to resolve the matter.

Videos

Much of the advice about choosing a photographer also applies to videos. Shop around and view sample videos. The Institute of Videography or the Association of Professional Videomakers will give advice and recommendations.

Having a wedding video made is now very popular, but you should ask your minister or registrar for permission to record the ceremony. Remember, this can have an impact on the fees charged by organists and choirs because of performing and copyright laws.

The average spent by couples on a wedding video is about £350, but a professional video will probably cost from £500 to £800. There should really be two camera operators and afterwards the video will need considerable editing. To produce a two-hour video with untidy shots edited out takes roughly a day. To produce a better quality video, shorter but more entertaining, takes considerably longer.

You can also hire a professional camera and ask a friend to do the filming for you, but you may not be as pleased with the finished product. To hire a professional camera for a weekend costs about £100 and the Institute of Videography and the Association of Professional Videomakers will be able to recommend equipment and companies.

THE VIDEO

- ✔ Do ensure that the video maker has professional indemnity insurance.
- ✔ Do make sure that the videographer is using a professional, not a domestic, camera (often the cheaper ones use domestic equipment).
- ✔ Do view samples of work.
- ✔ Do be clear about exactly what you want.
- ✔ Do make sure your video operator has a special licence to cover copyright laws (e.g. for hymns and service text).
- ✔ Do consider a video if a very close relative or friend is unable to attend your wedding.

11 FLOWERS

When anyone thinks of weddings, one of the first
images to spring to mind is that of flowers. Their
association with marriage ceremonies goes back
centuries – in medieval times, flowers and herbs were
thought to ward off evil spirits and more recently
they have been used to add scent and romance.

Wedding flowers may include a bridal bouquet
and posies for the bridesmaids, possibly floral
headdresses, buttonholes for the groom, best man,
ushers, mothers and fathers of the bride and groom,
and other family members. There are usually flowers
at the ceremony – in the entrance, in the aisle, at the
pew ends – and at the reception – by the entrance,
near the receiving line, as room decorations, table
centrepieces and next to the cake.

When choosing a florist:

- Preferably pick a local florist on personal
  recommendation.
- Shop around for the best deals.
- Visit florists to see whether you like the types of
  flowers and arrangements they have in stock.
- Ask to see pictures of past work.

- Avoid florists who show you photos of standard bouquets or decorations and who won't be flexible.
- Discuss your ideas and preferences and see how they respond. A good florist should be able to add to your ideas and present you with something better than you originally had in mind.

VISITING THE FLORIST

✓ Do take along pictures of your own and the bridesmaids' dresses, together with any swatches of material.

✓ Do take along magazine cuttings of designs for bouquets and arrangements you especially like.

✓ Do take photographs or sketches of the ceremony and reception venues.

✓ Do fully explain any colour schemes or other themes you may have for the wedding.

✓ Do tell the florist if there are any flowers you particularly like or dislike.

✓ Do ask for a written quote.

Book your florist at least four months in advance – allow longer if your wedding is at Christmas or near St Valentine's Day.

To cut costs, choose flowers that are in season and a florist close to the venues to keep delivery charges to a minimum.

The Flowers and Plants Association can offer help with all aspects of choosing wedding flowers. They will recommend a florist nearby, tell you which flowers are available in each season and the best buys for the month, as well as information about specific flowers (colours, scents and so on), plus suggestions about mixing and matching. They can even answer questions about the symbolism of flowers.

Send a stamped addressed envelope requesting information to:

Flowers and Plants Association
Covent House
New Covent Garden Market
London SW8 5NX
• www.flowers.org.uk

Seasonal flowers

Many flowers are now available all year round – at a price. The following is a guide to which flowers are most readily available and abundant at different times of the year.

Spring Wax flower (*Chamaelaucium*), lily of the valley, lilac, broom, snowball tree (*Viburnum opulus 'roseum'*), guelder rose (*Viburnum opulus*), some early flowering peonies, cherry, apple, lemon and orange blossom, African corn lily, cow parsley (from late spring) and bulb flowers such as daffodil, narcissus, tulip, hyacinth, bluebell and grape hyacinth.

Summer Lemon and orange blossom, cow parsley, meadowsweet, honeysuckle, jasmine, peony, phlox, stock, sweet william, marguerite, sweet pea, clarkia, *Alchemilla mollis*, campanula, goldenrod, lilies, allium, poppy, lavender, sunflower, tuberose, monkshood, hydrangea, agapanthus, passion flower, euphorbia, ranunculus and a host of other flowers in a palette of shades and colours.

Autumn Goldenrod, love-lies-bleeding, hypericum (St John's wort), yarrow, late-flowering honeysuckle, red-hot poker, crocosmia, dahlia, gladiolus, globe thistle, Chinese aster, globe amaranth, scabious, sedum, stonecrop, late-flowering sunflowers, zinnia, godetia, montbretia and a range of berries, attractive twigs and seedpods.

Winter Hellebore, snowdrop, early bulb flowers such as hyacinth, daffodil, tulip, narcissus and amaryllis, protea, kangaroo paw, winter jasmine, holly and other berries and twigs.

Available all year Rose, iris, arum lily, calla lily, other lily varieties, lisianthus, lysimachia, freesia, carnation, gerbera, baby's breath (gypsophila), iris, alstroemeria, anemone, chrysanthemum, September flower, snapdragon, orchid, ornamental pineapple, bird of paradise (strelitzia), statice.

Flowers for the bride and bridesmaids

As the bride, you should choose a bouquet to suit your personality and complement your dress. You should consider your favourite flowers and look for those whose fragrance, shape or colour you particularly enjoy.

You should only make decisions about flowers after you have chosen your dress, as the shape and detailing will influence your choice. If your dress is very elaborate, you may want a simple posy to balance your look, but a very elegant, classic-cut dress may demand an equally elegant, stylish bouquet.

Current trends for weddings include hand-tied bouquets and posies in delicate pastel shades and vividly exuberant, contrasting colours. Try lily of the valley mixed with grape hyacinths, tiny roses and stephanotis or pastel sweet peas for delicate, scented bouquets. Perfect pink peonies on their own or mixed with white arum lilies, *Alchemilla mollis*, bell-shaped lisianthus and cow parsley give a romantically soft but stunning look. Arum and calla lilies make wonderful sculptural bouquets and can look just as striking when only a few are carried. For bright jewelled colours, choose parrot tulips, orange and red arum or calla lilies, deep shades of fragrant roses, anemones and gerberas. Flowers can be mixed with trailing leaves, other greenery and berries, and tied with ribbons or raffia. Some florists add tiny crystals and even feathers.

Bridesmaids' bouquets should complement the colours of their dresses and are often a smaller, simpler version of the bride's bouquet. One option may be for the chief bridesmaid to carry a small posy to match the bride's while the others hold pretty bags.

Ask your bridesmaids to hand out dried rose petals for guests to throw instead of confetti. Fill paper cones with the petals and display them in wicker baskets for bridesmaids to carry round after the ceremony.

Headdresses

You may wish to include fresh flowers in your hair or as part of a headdress to harmonise with the flowers in your bouquet. Your florist and hairdresser should be able to advise both on ways to use flowers and on types which will last the longest. Flowers chosen should ideally look as fresh at the end of the day as they did at the start of the ceremony. One effective idea is to wire tiny rosebuds and thread these into your hair – a technique which could be used with many other flowers, individually and in small clusters.

If you'd like flowers in your hair but don't want to risk them wilting in the sunshine, you could look at tiaras and circlets made with delicate enamel flowers or consider silk. It is also possible to find unusual tiaras made from beautiful wax flowers.

HEADDRESSES

Enamel circlets and headdresses: Halo and Co.:
01283 704305

Wax floral tiaras: Jules & Arfor: 01304 364887

Buttonholes

These are worn by the groom, best man, ushers and both fathers. Buttonholes may be handed out to members of the two families and sometimes to every guest. Traditionally, they were always a carnation or rose, but the choice of flower is completely personal. You may want to coordinate with your chosen colour scheme or pick out one of the flowers from the bride's bouquet.

Always take advice from your florist about suitable flowers. You don't want anything that will quickly wither without water.

Corsages

These are more ornate buttonholes and usually comprise more than one flower head. They are worn by the two mothers and can either coordinate with the other flowers chosen for the day or simply complement their outfits.

Flowers for the ceremony
CHURCH WEDDINGS

For a church ceremony, flowers are most often placed at the church entrance, the pew ends, the chancel steps, the pulpit, lectern, windowsills and font. They are sometimes used to decorate pillars and placed on flower stands. You may have a very clear idea of the types and colours of flowers and the arrangements you want, but *always* speak to the church minister before ordering.

There may be restrictions, either because of the time of year and a particular religious festival, or because more than one wedding ceremony is taking place in the church that day. Different churches also have their own rules about where flowers may be placed. If there is another wedding party, ask the vicar for their telephone number and contact them to see if you can coordinate arrangements.

Some churches also have their own team of flower arrangers, in which case you should speak to the organiser to discuss any particular requests for flowers or colours. You will probably be asked to make a contribution towards the cost and even if not asked, you should offer a donation.

If you are given permission to arrange your own flowers, agree a time with the minister for their delivery and arrangement, and check exactly where you are allowed to place them. If you are keen to have floral decorations at the pew ends, check whether there are any special fittings – some churches will supply hooks (which must be returned) and most will not be happy for you to use drawing pins or nails. You may not have very long before the wedding ceremony to arrange your flowers, sometimes no more than an hour, and churches often stipulate that you take all floral arrangements away with you after the wedding. You might consider using them again at the reception – for instance, pew ends can make excellent table decorations.

FLOWERS AT CHURCH WEDDINGS
✓ Do check exactly what is allowed and accept any restrictions.
✓ Do discuss possible colours and flowers with the church flower arranger.
✓ Don't refuse to compromise.

CIVIL WEDDINGS
Many register offices and marriage rooms will already be decorated with fresh flowers. If not, check on the arrangements for providing your own. It is unlikely that you will be able to decorate very far ahead of your ceremony time.

For civil ceremonies elsewhere, find out whether flowers are included as part of the arrangement and

whether you can choose to provide your own.
Depending on the size of the room, two or three
impressive arrangements will probably be sufficient,
with one placed near the entrance.

Reception flowers

As with civil ceremonies, the reception venue may
organise flower arrangements for you. If so, find out
exactly what they provide and discuss choices. You
may be able to specify preferences and you should
certainly explain any colour theme.

At the reception, it is a good idea to decorate the
entrance and place an arrangement near to the
receiving line. Other large arrangements could be
positioned next to the table seating plan, near the
entrance to the dining room or marquee, and inside.
Flowers are usually set near to the wedding cake, but
this will depend on the style of the cake, and if
flowers already feature strongly in its design, it may
not be a good idea to place more nearby.

TABLE DECORATIONS

Floral table decorations also add to the atmosphere
you are trying to create and the colours and flowers
you choose will be important in setting the tone.
Cream and white roses and lilies are classically
traditional; roses, peonies, sweet peas and freesias in
pastel hues are gently romantic; while bright tulips,

gerberas, calla lilies and amaryllis can look modern and informal.

Choose lily of the valley, gardenias, stephanotis, orange and lemon blossom, hyacinths, lavender, rosemary, sweet peas, freesias and roses for their wonderful fragrance – try scattering lavender, rosebuds and petals on to tables to add to the scent. You can make the arrangements light and summery or vividly dramatic, and accent your choice of flowers with foliage, trailing leaves and twigs.

When choosing designs for table decorations, bear in mind that guests will want to be able to see one another across the tables.

HAYFEVER SUFFERERS

Allergies to pollen can be a real problem, especially for summer weddings. Some flowers have less effect on hayfever sufferers, including orchids, arum and calla lilies, irises, cornflowers and ranunculus. Most leaves, foliage, twigs and berries should also be safe choices.

Your florist will be able to help with further suggestions. Also contact the Flowers and Plants Association.

Fake flowers

Another alternative for hayfever sufferers, and also for those who want their flowers to last, is to choose good-quality silk or freeze-dried flowers. These could be used for all the flower arrangements and also for the bride's and bridesmaids' posies and hair.

For fabulously real fake flowers, try Bloom, tel: 01570 481160, and check bride magazines for other sources.

Delivery

Bouquets, posies and buttonholes are usually delivered to the bride's parents' home on the morning of the wedding. Occasionally they need to be collected, so always check before the day.

The florist will need to know exactly where and when to set up any other arrangements and decorations and will need specific details and addresses for delivery.

It is one of the best man's duties to make sure the bride and groom, the parents and ushers all have their flowers on the day.

FLOWER DELIVERIES

✔ Do telephone or visit the florist a few days before the wedding to confirm arrangements and make sure everything is ready.

Flowers to say thank you

Even when they are just helping out and not paying for the whole event, most mothers (of the bride and groom) put a great deal of hard work and effort into helping to make their children's wedding day special. Presenting them with a bouquet of flowers each at the reception is a good way to say thank you – for everything.

It should be possible to arrange these with your florist, but make sure they are delivered to the reception venue.

- **www.0800-Blossoms.com** is a website which will deliver last-minute bouquets, gifts and champagne.

Preserving your bouquet

People have been drying and preserving flowers since ancient Egyptian times and there are various methods to preserve all or part of the bouquet.

DRYING

Either hang flowers upside down in a cool place for about a month or place them in a box filled with silica gel crystals and leave until all the moisture has been absorbed by the silica. You can also press flowers individually by laying them between sheets of absorbent paper and weighting them down. After about two months you can use the pressed flowers to make a picture or collage.

There are professional companies which will press and frame flowers or preserve whole posies for you.

PRESERVING FLOWERS

The Flower Framing Company: 020 8741 0077

Pressed for Time: 01489 574668

Pressed Flower Design: 01273 424299

Petals & Lace: 01371 873986

FREEZE-DRYING

This sounds a new idea but Andean Indians have been practising a form of freeze-drying for centuries.

Flowers should really be pre-treated and rehydrated before they are freeze-dried. Bouquets are photographed and then taken apart so each flower can be individually treated to keep its colour and shape. After freeze-drying, the flowers should then be treated again. All these steps are necessary to ensure a perfectly preserved posy. The flowers will then retain their natural colour and shape and last longer.

There are very few experts and you should contact them at least two months before a wedding to make arrangements.

Paying for flowers

Traditionally, the groom pays for the bride's bouquet and other flowers for the wedding party. The bride's family pays for flowers for the ceremony and reception.

12 THE WEDDING CAKE

The wedding cake is often the visual focal point of a reception and traditionally is a symbol of fertility and marital happiness. We may have abandoned the practice of crumbling cake over the bride's head, but the ritual of the bride and groom making the first cut into the cake as a sign of their shared future continues.

Wedding cakes used to be round or square, with two to four tiers, and were almost always rich fruit cake iced in white and draped with sugar-paste roses and ivy. Many couples still opt for this traditional style, based, it is said, on the unusual shape of St Bride's Church spire. However, wedding cakes now come in all shapes, sizes and colours. You may serve a white chocolate extravaganza, a summery lemon or passion cake, or a dark chocolate or meringue confection, and the cake is just as likely to look like your reception venue or a pyramid of flowers. You can be as creative as you like, with both flavours and shapes. The wedding cake can be fun or an edible work of art that is hopefully also delicious to eat.

Generally, there is a move towards making cakes and decorations as unique and individual as possible, and although tiered cakes are still favoured, most are stacked directly on the tier below or placed on top of flowers instead of plastic pillars.

Chocolate wedding cakes are now extremely popular and tiers supported by rosebud rings can look stunning. Another trend is for individual sponge cakes, piled high and decorated with fresh flowers, or iced and tied with ribbons. These can be served as dessert with fruit coulis and mixed berries.

Another popular style is to make the wedding cake look like a stack of presents. Each square tier is iced to look like a gift-wrapped present tied with a ribbon that may be either real ribbon or made from icing. These 'presents' are then stacked one on top of the other with the ribbons cascading down the sides. Themed wedding cakes are also increasingly common – for instance, sea-shell decorations for a beach or seaside wedding.

Square cakes are better value than round ones and are easier to slice.

KEEPING ONE TIER OF WEDDING CAKE

Some couples like to keep the smallest, top tier of wedding cake for their first child's christening or to celebrate their first wedding anniversary. If this idea appeals, you should opt for a fruit cake, as this is the only type of cake that will remain fresh (and may even improve with age). The fruit will probably seep through and discolour the icing, but the cake can be re-iced when you want to eat it. Wrapped carefully, a rich fruit cake can last for several years.

The classic wedding-cake shape with successively smaller tiers, decorative icing and festoons first appeared at the marriage of one of Queen Victoria's daughters in 1859. In fact, only the base layer was actually cake; the other tiers were sugar paste, and the layers were stacked like hatboxes. The first wedding cake composed entirely of cake was made for the wedding of Victoria's son, Prince Leopold, in 1882. Pillars separating the tiers did not appear until the beginning of the 20th century.

Traditionally, the cake is positioned at the centre of the top table at a sit-down reception or in the middle of the food platters at a buffet. More often today, it is set on a special display stand close by the top table. It is placed in front of the newlywed couple only when the time comes for it to be cut.

The cake-cutting usually follows the speeches and toasts and marks the end of the formalities. After the couple have made the first cut, the cake is taken away to be sliced professionally. The cake should be large enough for every guest to receive a piece and for slices to be sent to those who couldn't be there. If the meal is at lunchtime, the cake may be served later with coffee.

Make sure you have a sharp knife to hand for the cake-cutting. A cake slice is also essential if you are serving the cake yourselves.

Cake-makers

There are many specialist cake-makers, both companies and individuals, and you may even find that the hotel or reception venue or your caterers will make a wedding cake for you.

Looking through bride magazines is a good starting point for inspiration on design, and you will also find the contact numbers for companies making cakes.

THE WEDDING CAKE

✓ Do ask for friends' recommendations.
✓ Do visit several suppliers before making a decision.
✓ Do ask to see a portfolio of the types of cakes available.
✓ Do ask to taste a sample of the cake you are ordering.
✓ Do order at least three months in advance.

Always ask for a written quote and check that it includes any pillars necessary, display trays or stands, and any other decorations. For a simple, traditional three-tier cake you should expect to pay at least £150. For a more elaborate and unusual design you could easily pay double this amount. There are also many people who run their own businesses making wedding cakes from home and they are often excellent value for money. As with a larger company, ask to see photographs of previous work and, if possible, taste a sample. Word of mouth is the best way of finding independent local makers.

The finished cake is usually delivered to the caterers (or reception venue if they are organising food) the day before the wedding. But you should be very clear about the delivery details and make sure that each separate tier is carefully packed in its own box. The cake should not be assembled until the day of the wedding, when it should be decorated ready for display.

Home-made cakes

Making the cake yourself can be a good way to save money. If you are planning a fruit cake, you should start baking about three months before the wedding and ideally the cake should stand for six to nine weeks before icing.

With all the other wedding preparations, you may feel you don't have the time to bake, ice and decorate a cake yourself and there may be a friend or relative who would be willing to do it for you.

TIP: A word of warning: intricate decoration and a professional finish are tricky even for a competent cake-maker. An amateur cake can be a major source of disaster and at least you can complain to a professional if something goes wrong.

For an elegant home-made wedding cake, cover each cake with smooth fondant icing and then stack progressively smaller tiers directly on top of one another. Don't attempt fiddly details but pipe a simple rim of icing around the joins, or secure narrow ribbons around the base of each layer. Then decorate on the day with fresh flowers.

It was traditional in some countries to hide a ring and other tokens in the wedding cake. Whoever found the ring was said to be the next to be married. Finding a token was thought to ensure happiness for the coming year.

13 WEDDING CARS & TRANSPORT

At one time it was common for the bride and groom to walk to their wedding together. Nowadays, most rely on cars to get them to the church on time. There are usually two wedding cars at a traditional wedding. The first takes the bride's mother and bridesmaids to the ceremony and the second takes the bride and her father (or whoever is giving her away). This second car later takes the bride and groom on to the reception and the first takes the bride's parents and the bridesmaids. The bride's family usually organise these cars.

The travel arrangements generally are the responsibility of the best man and certainly on the day he should be overseeing, making certain that everything runs smoothly and to time. It is the best man who will take the groom to the ceremony, preferably arriving ahead of the bride's mother and the bridesmaids. He should be the last to leave after the ceremony and is often helped by the ushers. He then takes the car on to the reception, having first made sure that all the guests are taken care of and no one is left stranded. The best man also organises the bride and groom's transport away from the reception and on to their honeymoon if necessary.

What means of transport?

With the revival of interest in traditional 'big' weddings and couples' desire to make a dramatic entrance and exit, the choice of wedding transport has never been wider.

A professional car hire company can help your wedding day run smoothly. This is one of the most popular options and the average cost is about £300. Many couples still opt for a classic Rolls-Royce or Bentley in white or black but these are far from the only vehicles available. There are vintage cars, American Cadillacs and Mercedes and Daimler limousines; there are also post-war classic cars like the *Inspector Morse* Mark II Jaguar; and it is not unknown for couples to arrive on tractors, fire engines and steam trains.

For a romantically traditional approach, you could hire a horse and carriage. This is really only suitable for summer weddings and you need to book well in advance – up to two years is not unusual. Costs vary from around £400 to around £800, depending on the style of carriage, number of horses, etc.

You could organise a convoy of cars to ferry your guests from the ceremony to the reception, and it is also possible to hire a fleet of black cabs or a double-decker.

CAR HIRE FIRMS

American Classic Hire Co.: 01895 421962

American 50s Convertibles: 01268 735914 (pink and white convertibles from 1959 and 1960)

Bespokes Classics: 020 7833 8000, or

• **www.bespokes.co.uk** (range includes classic Mark II Jaguars and self-drive sports cars)

Capital Carriages: 01277 372082

Carriages Vehicle Agency: 01737 353926 (for your very own Batmobile and others)

Cars of Character: 01494 792013 (more than 1,000 cars nationwide)

East London Coaches: 01708 731088

Fleetwood Classic Limousines: 020 7700 8403

Greens Car Hire: 020 8692 9200

Lord Cars Limited: 01707 262520, or

• **www.lordcars.co.uk**

Northern Sports Car Hire: 0800 052 5066, or

• **www.sportscarhire.net**

Preston's Wedding Cars: 020 8391 5996

Regency Carriages: 01494 481004, or

• **www.regencycarriages.co.uk**

Other useful websites for wedding transport include:

• **www.weddingcars.co.uk**

- www.qm4.com
- www.wedding-service.co.uk

HIRING WEDDING TRANSPORT

✔ Do ask for friends' recommendations – there are advantages to using a local firm.

✔ Do make sure you know exactly what you are hiring.

✔ Do, if possible, visit the company in person and look at the specific vehicle that will be used for your wedding.

✔ Do check what is included in the price – if it's a chauffeur-driven car there should not be an extra charge for the driver, and any ribbons or decorations should be included in the price (some companies even throw in complimentary champagne).

✔ Do consider the size of your wedding dress when choosing transport – some dresses are made from oceans of material and require a great deal of space.

✔ Do check on how easy it is to get in and out of the vehicle.

✔ Do check on contingency plans and substitute vehicles should anything go wrong.

✔ Do get a written quote.

✔ Do ask for written confirmation of the booking and date and time you are expecting the transport. Make sure they have all the relevant addresses: home, ceremony and reception.

✔ Do book ahead – give as much notice as possible.

Economies

Borrowing a classic or sporty car from a willing relative or close friend for the day is one way to cut costs. They may even offer to drive it for you. Another way to economise is to hire only one car. One of the ushers could take over responsibility for chauffeuring the bride's mother and bridesmaids to the ceremony and you could recruit friends to help guests without their own transport.

If you are relying on other people, it is a good idea to make absolutely sure everyone knows who they are responsible for and to have one or two reserve cars on the day. You should also offer to reimburse costs.

Hiring self-drive cars is usually less expensive than opting for chauffeur-driven ones and a friend may be willing to stand in as driver for the day.

PARKING

✓ Do check parking arrangements for the ceremony and reception.

✓ Do make alternative arrangements if parking is tricky nearby.

✓ Do let guests know about any parking restrictions.

✓ Do send out specific parking instructions with invitations.

✓ Do send out location maps and directions for the

ceremony and reception (preferably with guests'
invitations). Either draw them clearly yourself or
photocopy a local map.

14 WEDDING PRESENTS & LISTS

The practice of guests giving wedding gifts has replaced the old custom of bringing fruits to the newlyweds to encourage fertility; the gifts were seen as a way to help the couple set up home together.

Sending out a wedding list with your invitation used to be frowned upon. However, times change, and the practice is now so widespread, and so popular with guests as well as the bride and groom, that there is no stigma attached to enclosing a note of the company holding your wedding list, together with their telephone number or email address. The first company to offer a bridal gift service was the General Trading Company in London, as long ago as the 1920s. At that time, newspapers published lists of presents given and the givers.

The wedding list has moved on from simply being a way to furnish a new home with basic equipment. Many couples live together before marriage and gift lists can be a way of acquiring items you wouldn't buy yourself, upgrading things you already have or treating yourself to something unusual or luxurious.

Company and store wedding lists

The most popular and easiest way to compile a wedding list is to place it with a shop or department store. To draw up a list, visit the store and make a note of any items that interest you. Many stores have branches across the country and may also have a catalogue which you can browse at home. You should think about placing your list with a store about eight to ten weeks before the wedding.

Guests can choose gifts by telephone, through the internet or by visiting in person. The store will manage your wedding list as part of the service, so when an item has been bought, it will automatically be removed from the list. You will be kept informed as to who has bought each gift so that you know who to thank.

If you don't want to restrict your list to just one shop or store, there are now several companies who will compile and handle a wedding list for you. Although using a company gives you greater flexibility, they generally charge a fee for the service, whereas placing your list with a store is free.

COMPANIES OFFERING WEDDING LIST SERVICES

The Gift List Company: 020 7384 8400, or
• **www.thegiftlist.co.uk**
The Present Connection:
• **www.present.co.uk**

Wedding List Services: 020 7978 1118, or

• **www.wedding.co.uk**

The Wedding Shop: 020 7384 8400, or

• **www.theweddingshoponline.com**

Wedding List Company: 020 7584 1222, or

• **www.theweddinglist.co.uk**

Letting people know

You may not have finally decided what to do about a wedding list when you send out your invitations or you may prefer not to appear to be asking for a present by including a note. Many guests will assume you do have a list and will probably ask about arrangements. Unless it is a close friend who knows your taste very well, most people prefer to choose something from a list that they can be sure you'll appreciate.

Some stores will give you cards to send out with your invitations explaining where your list is held.

WEDDING PRESENTS

✔ Do include a wide range of presents at a range of prices.

✔ Do list some cheaper items.

✔ Do ask for fun things – a wacky loo brush or a designer lemon squeezer, if that's what you want.

✔ Do remember that wedding presents are meant to last for a long time, so include some items which will stand the test of time – for instance, dinner plates that you

will still like in ten years, good-quality saucepans and knives.
✓ Do give some thought both to what you need and to what you would like before visiting a store or drawing up a final list.
✓ Do send a handwritten thank you in acknowledgement of a gift as soon as possible.
✓ Don't leave out expensive items – guests may club together to buy you something special.
✓ Don't worry about what are considered traditional wedding gifts – include what you want.

Compiling your list

The main gift areas that couples consider when compiling their wedding list are:

- china and glassware
- bedlinen
- lighting
- garden furniture and tools
- bathroom accessories and linen
- electrical equipment
- kitchen equipment (including knives and saucepans)
- cutlery and other dining accessories
- miscellaneous items such as photo frames, rugs, vases, candlesticks and cushions
- plants, trees, luggage, personalised scents etc.

GIFT LIST

✗ Don't include personal items such as clothing or jewellery on a wedding list.

Some stores with online facilities will allow you to manage the gift list yourself, which means you can check and amend your list whenever you want. The table on pages 226-227 gives telephone numbers and website addresses for stores throughout Britain.

Delivery

You will usually have a choice about whether you want wedding presents delivered before the wedding or even on the wedding day. Guests may also choose to collect and deliver their gift personally.

The convention was always to display gifts, but if you are leaving immediately for honeymoon you might prefer a store to hold on to them until your return.

WEDDING PRESENT DELIVERY

✓ Do arrange when and where the gifts should be delivered with the store.

✓ Do get confirmation of the arrangements in writing.

✓ Do be very specific about addresses and times.

WEDDING GIFT SERVICES CHECKLIST

Delivery service – some are free, always check
with the individual store ☐

Gift-wrapping service ☐

Gift vouchers ☐

Discounts on gifts ☐

Internet list ☐

Extra gifts or incentives for the couple ☐

Occasional promotions or special offers ☐

Travel vouchers

If you prefer the idea of guests contributing towards
the cost of your honeymoon rather than buying
conventional wedding presents, contact British
Airways Travel Shops, tel: 0845 606 0747, or
• **www.britishairwaysholidays.co.uk**. They have
vouchers for a range of prices which can be used as
full or part payment for flights and holidays. Eurostar
also offers this service, tel: 0870 5186186, or
• **www.eurostar.com**.

Wedding websites can also be very helpful when
compiling a gift list. Check:
• **www.wedding-service.co.uk**
• **www.confetti.co.uk**
• **www.all-about-weddings.co.uk**
• **www.hitched.co.uk**

Compiling your own wedding list

If you decide you would prefer to draw up your wedding list yourself rather than relying on a specific store or the services of a company, the basic rules remain the same. Make notes of everything you would like and make sure you are very specific. Include the manufacturer's name, the model number, the preferred colour and the price. It is also helpful to include a suggested stockist.

Traditionally, it is always the bride's mother who circulates and coordinates the list, but you could also ask a good friend or your chief bridesmaid. You should include a note asking guests to check with whoever is handling the list before making their final choice and buying anything.

Refer to the wedding websites for help and inspiration when thinking about a gift list. Bride magazines are also useful sources for ideas, as are home and interior magazines.

FURTHER READING

Setting Up Home by Lorrie Mack (Carlton Books, £16.99)

Space Clearing by Denise Linn (Rider, £7.99)

Try **www.focusdoitall.co.uk** for advice on all practical aspects of decorating and DIY.

SOME STORES OFFERING A WEDDING GIFT LIST SERVICE OR ONLINE GIFT-BUYING SERVICE

Contact	Location
Allders 020 8256 7000	nationwide • www.allders.co.uk
Argos 0870 600 2525	nationwide/catalogue • www.argos.co.uk
Debenhams 020 7580 3000	nationwide • www.debenhams.com
Designers Guild 020 7893 7400	London
Divertimenti 020 7581 8065	London • www.divertimenti.co.uk
Edinburgh Crystal 01968 672244	nationwide • www.edinburgh-crystal.com
Fenwicks 01227 766866 0116 255 3322 0191 232 5100	 Canterbury Leicester Newcastle
General Trading Company 01285 652314 020 7730 0411	 Cirencester London
Habitat 0845 601 0740	nationwide • www.habitat.net

Contact	Location
Harrods 020 7225 6500	London • www.harrods.com
Heal's 020 7636 1666	London • www.heals.co.uk
House of Fraser 020 7963 2000	nationwide
Jenners 0131 225 2442	Edinburgh • www.jenners.com
John Lewis 0845 600 2202	nationwide • www.johnlewis.com
Liberty 020 7734 1234	London/nationwide • www.liberty.co.uk
Marks & Spencer 0870 608 0505	nationwide • www.marksandspencer.com
Purves & Purves 020 7580 8223	London • www.purves.co.uk
Selfridges 020 7318 3395	London • www.selfridges.co.uk

Insurance

The total value of the wedding presents you receive will probably be a shock and you should check that your household contents insurance covers them. It is sensible to make sure your gifts are covered against accident, loss, theft and damage while away from your home, especially if the gifts are to be displayed at the reception or left at your parents' home, for instance, while you are away.

You can take out special wedding insurance, which will offer various levels of cover.

INSURANCE
Ecclesiastical Direct: 0800 336622
Country Mutual Insurance Brokers: 0118 957 5491
Hine Insurance Brokers Ltd: 0161 438 0000
Methodist Insurance: 0161 833 9696
E & L Insurance Services: 0870 742 3700

Exchanging gifts

Legally, you are entitled to a full refund for an item only if it is faulty. The fact that it is the wrong colour or you have more than one of them doesn't really count, although if you have a receipt or other proof of purchase you should be given your money back. Most large stores do operate a goodwill policy and in practice will change an item simply because you don't want it. If something is faulty you are expected to return it within a reasonable period of time and, of course, a wedding present might have been purchased some time before the wedding, or indeed at another branch. Again, you have to rely on the store manager's discretion, but it is worth pointing out that it was a wedding gift and hinting that you are usually a loyal customer of the store in question.

If your wedding list was held by a store or company, they will have a record of a gift's sale and changing it should be easy.

Should all else fail, several of the wedding websites offer a wedding gift swap service which might be worth checking.

Try: • www.webwedding.co.uk

Saying thank you

As soon as you receive a gift, or have been notified that one has been selected from your list, send handwritten thank-you notes. (Pre-printed cards are not really acceptable.)

If you have received any cheques or gift tokens, it is polite to say what you plan to buy with them and let the sender know their token is appreciated.

When signing informal letters as husband and wife, the woman's name always comes first.

When you cancel or postpone your wedding

Guests should be informed as soon as possible.
You don't have to explain yourselves or give reasons
– a simple note stating that the wedding has been
cancelled or postponed, including a possible future
date, is sufficient. If the wedding is cancelled, gifts
should be returned immediately.

15 COUNTDOWN TO THE BIG DAY

All the major planning decisions have been taken. You know what type of wedding you want and where the ceremony is to be held. You have found the perfect reception venue and discovered your dream dress. Flowers have been arranged and a photographer booked. You have considered music and readings, mulled over the menus and creative cakes, tasted the wine and road-tested the Rolls.

Surely all you have to do now is turn up on the day? In a perfect world, of course, that would be exactly how it would happen. There are, however, lots of things for the bride and groom to be thinking about on the wedding day – and lots more things for their support teams of family, bridesmaids, best man, etc. to be thinking about.

Now is the time for fine-tuning the arrangements, checking on progress and paying attention to detail. Look for those extra-special ingredients that will add the finishing touches. Involve your best man and chief bridesmaid and ask them to help. Have fun with good friends and enjoy each other's company. The countdown to the big day has begun.

Presents from the bride and groom

It is customary for the bride and groom to buy presents for the other members of the wedding party to say thank you, and to show their appreciation for the help and support they have received. The wedding will, hopefully, be a happy occasion for the bridesmaids, best man and ushers and one which they want to remember. A carefully chosen gift is an extra memento of the day. Gifts are usually presented at the reception – at appropriate moments during the toasts and speeches – or before the wedding – at the rehearsal or at a pre-wedding drinks party or meal.

Presents can be anything you think will be appreciated. Many couples opt for something to keep and jewellery is a popular choice.

CHIEF BRIDESMAID OR MATRON OF HONOUR

If the chief bridesmaid is older than the other bridesmaids, you might consider giving her a special gift as a token of the extra effort she has made on your behalf for the wedding, and also because she is probably your best friend or sister and you've shared a great deal together over the years. The same is true for the matron of honour, especially as she will be the only female attendant.

A maid of honour becomes a matron of honour if she is married. And a chief bridesmaid is called a maid or matron of honour if she is the only female attendant to the bride. Their duties are identical, except for the fact that the chief bridesmaid will also be responsible for the other bridesmaids, especially if they are younger.

Present ideas for bridesmaids, young and old, include necklaces, bracelets, lockets, pendants, jewellery to be worn on the wedding day with their bridesmaid dresses, earrings, photo frames, perfume.

BEST MAN
The present for the best man should also be something special. You will have known him for years (all his life if he's your brother), and being a best man entails a long list of responsibilities. The smooth running of events on your wedding day will depend to a great degree on his contribution.

Present ideas include cufflinks, tie pin, watch, wallet, silk tie, briefcase, glasses.

USHERS
You may wish to acknowledge the help given by your ushers.

Suitable presents to say thank you include bottles of wine or champagne, flowers, or a fun memento of the day.

PARENTS
Even when couples are paying for their own wedding,

they often choose to give something to their parents as a token of gratitude for everything they have done over the years. The gifts can be given at the reception as part of the groom's speech and toast, or before the wedding day.

Presents for parents can be as simple as flowers for the mothers and a favourite bottle for the fathers, or as extravagant as a weekend away. You know what your parents would enjoy, from theatre tickets or a game of golf, to a silver photo frame or decanter. Whatever you decide, parents are sure to appreciate the gesture.

COUNTDOWN FOR THE BRIDE

The key elements of your wedding outfit will already have been chosen and you will know the overall look you are trying to achieve. Now is the time to search for the perfect accessories and extras that can make such a difference, both for you and for your bridesmaids.

Hair

Perhaps you knew exactly what to do with your hair and what headdress to wear as soon as you found your dress. It is more likely, though, that you will have some idea of what you like but be unsure either of what suits you best or how to achieve the style you want.

It is a good idea to talk to a hairstylist as soon as possible. You could choose a wedding hair specialist, your usual hairdresser or one specially recommended by a friend. They will be able to advise you and suggest the correct products to condition your hair.

Describe your dress, or better still show them a photograph, and discuss the types of style you prefer and what would work best with your dress. A good stylist should be able to give you a realistic idea of what can be achieved with your particular hair.

HAIR STYLE TIPS

Hair should match the tone of the dress:

- For a detailed dress with a full skirt, go for an elaborate, glamorous hairstyle.
- For a simple dress, keep hair sleek and naturally stylish.
- For a strapless dress or one with a scooped neckline, take hair up into a French pleat.

HAIR

✔ Do look in bride magazines. They are packed with tips and information on products and hair accessories, and will point you towards new trends, current ideas and styles.

✔ Do choose a style that accentuates your best features.

✘ Don't choose a look that is vastly different from usual (if you normally wear your hair up in a French pleat, go for a perfected or more interesting version; if your hair is naturally wavy, accentuate the curls).

✘ Don't choose a headdress until you've found your hairdresser. They should be able to advise what will suit your face shape and hair type – basically say what will work for you.

Tiaras look wonderful on sleek, short or layered haircuts, but they can also work well when long hair is drawn back into a simple chignon. Fresh flowers look stunning on most brides. You can choose single flowers on wires, floral circlets or hairbands, or use flowers to emphasise or soften your hairstyle. Your florist will recommend flowers which will last – freesias, roses, gypsophila and orchids are usually reliable choices.

Countdown to perfect hair

Six months before the wedding is the time to start really looking after your hair. Condition it regularly and, even if you are growing it longer, have regular trims and conditioning treatments.

HAIR PRACTICALITIES

✔ Do check how long everything takes. This will be important when you come to work out a timetable for getting ready on your wedding day.

✔ Do try taking vitamin B – leading trichologists recommend it as particularly good for healthy hair and it's helpful for stress too.

✔ Do try to have a perm done about eight weeks before your wedding, if this is your planned style.

✔ Do book an appointment for colour or highlights no more than a month before the wedding day.

✔ Do experiment with different styles.

✔ Do book a practice session with your stylist when you have finally made a decision.

✔ Do book a final, extra practice session just before the wedding, or when you are having your final trim. This is the case even if you are doing your own hair on the day and the stylist is just teaching you how.

✓ Do practise – at least twice. If a friend is helping you, make sure she knows what you want. You want to find out before the wedding morning if your chosen style is not going to work.

✗ Don't take risks. Avoid permanent colours if you're not used to them. Highlights are a safer option, enhancing your natural colour but not making a drastic colour change.

✗ Don't leave the final trim until just before the wedding; always have hair cut about two or three weeks earlier, to give it time to soften.

PRACTICE SESSION OR DUMMY RUN

When you think you know what wedding hairstyle to go for, book a dummy run with your hairstylist. Make sure he or she knows exactly what you want and what your dress looks like. Take along your veil if you are wearing one, as well as your headdress. If you have chosen one incorporating fresh flowers, this may not be possible, but show your stylist a photograph or describe it very clearly. It may be that silk flowers or pins could be used to give the general effect.

Afterwards, go home and try on your wedding dress to make sure you are happy with the result. You should also feel confident that your hair will look good throughout the day. Avoid anything that is wonderful to begin with but will require constant attention. You should be able to forget all about your hair after it is styled on the day.

HAIRDRESSERS

Some big-name hairdressers offer special wedding packages for brides' and bridesmaids' hair.

You may decide that you would like your hairstylist to come to you on your wedding morning. Many are quite happy to do this.

HAIR APPOINTMENTS
✔ Do book well ahead.
✔ Do remember you may have to pay them for a whole morning, or half a day, not simply for the time taken to style your hair.

Hen party

A hen party should ideally be arranged about a month before your wedding and there should certainly be at least a week between hen party and ceremony. Chief bridesmaids usually plan the event, just as the best man takes over the organisation of the stag night. Traditionally, these were always separate parties – the bride with her friends and the groom with his. Nowadays, it is perfectly acceptable to combine the two if you have joint friends, and many of the standard activities chosen for hen and stag nights tend to be the same. The trend seems to be that hen nights are more riotous than they used to be, while stag nights are becoming better behaved, with the end result that the two are often very similar (with a few notable exceptions).

ORGANISATION

Although the details of the hen night may be a surprise, most brides prefer to make suggestions for the guest list. It is usually close friends, family and bridesmaids who are invited and the list can include members of the groom's family. Some brides like to invite their mothers, but there are no real rules other than it is normal to include only people who are going to the wedding.

The hen party may be an indulgent day with friends having beauty treatments and generally spoiling yourselves at a health and beauty club, a wild night out, a weekend or even a week away with your best girlfriends, or a nostalgic girly night in with food, wine, videos and old photos.

HEN PARTY ORGANISATION
✓ Do liaise with the bride for the guest list.
✓ Do check possible and impossible dates.
✓ Do make sure the bride and other guests will be happy and comfortable with what you are planning.
✓ Do remember the hen party should be a chance for the bride to relax with old friends and have fun before the wedding.

✔ Do budget carefully.

✔ Don't arrange anything outrageous if you know the bride will hate it.

HEN PARTY COSTS

✔ Do show the costs to the other 'hens' and make sure they agree.

✔ Do ask for a deposit from everyone.

Costs obviously vary according to your plans, but they can include:

- Travel
- Food and drink
- Entertainment
- Accommodation
- Special outfits and prizes (if you're plotting any fun/silly party games)

PRESENTS

In the US, most brides are given a bridal shower. Held at a good friend's house, all the bride's closest and oldest girlfriends gather together. The bride is 'showered' with gifts. These differ from wedding presents in being for the bride personally, and typically include lingerie, perfume, bath oils, jewellery, cashmere and silk. There may also be some more practical domestic presents.

The practice has not caught on here, but the hen party is still an ideal time to give the bride fun presents or mementoes of your friendship, bridal gifts like a garter or jokey presents like a personal marriage survival kit – the ingredients can be as imaginative or exotic as you like.

IDEAS FOR HEN PARTIES

Everyone has their favourite bars, restaurants and clubs, and their own ideas about what would make a perfect hen party.

Bride magazines often have unusual ideas and are a good source of addresses.

Wedding websites are also worth a look. A particularly good one is • **www.weddingguide.co.uk**. This has suggestions for venues, party ideas, games and even readers' thoughts on suitable fancy dress.

The Weekend Company, tel: 0115 989 9889, organises activity weekends, including hen and stag parties.

Treating yourself

This is also the time when you should be getting plenty of sleep – a good reason for arranging your hen party early – and indulging in all those beauty treats and treatments you don't always find time for.

PRE-WEDDING TREATS

- ✔ Do have regular facials.
- ✔ Do take time for a manicure.
- ✔ Do have a pedicure.
- ✔ Do ask a professional to pluck your eyebrows.
- ✔ Do book an aromatherapy massage.
- ✔ Do eat well – lots of healthy fruit and vegetables.
- ✔ Do drink plenty of water – it really improves your skin and general well-being.

Going-away outfit

With your main outfit for the day finalised, you can concentrate on choosing a going-away outfit to change into when you are leaving the reception. Your choice will depend upon your own style and whether you are leaving immediately on honeymoon.

Take your best friend with you on a shopping spree. You could combine the trip with your final wedding-dress fitting, a wedding make-up lesson or choosing some sexy underwear.

Present for the groom

This is not essential but some brides like to give the groom a present just before the wedding, especially if he is not going to wear a ring. This could be a permanent keepsake but could equally well be a surprise booking for a weekend away later in the year or a course that you know he would enjoy.

Family planning

If you don't already have this covered, make an appointment with your GP. Some surgeries run their own family planning clinics where you can ask for advice or information on what is best for you.

Spend time with your mum

Your mother would probably enjoy a day out with you. Perhaps you could help her accessorise her wedding outfit, have lunch, shop or go for some other girls' treat. Your wedding is a big day for your mum too and she will appreciate spending some time alone with you.

COUNTDOWN FOR THE GROOM

Just as for the bride, all the main planning decisions will have been made and now is the time to attend to the details.

Wedding outfit

You will know by now what style suit or wedding clothes you are wearing but there is still time to look for the perfect tie or cravat to match your waistcoat and to buy a new pair of shoes, shirt or cufflinks. It is also worth thinking about what you are going to change into after the reception. Everyone discusses the bride's going-away outfit, but there is no reason why the groom should not look just as stylish. You might also consider splashing out on some new clothes for your honeymoon.

Hair

Hair should be in top condition and well cut.

HAIR PRACTICALITIES

✔ Do have your hair cut about two weeks before the wedding. This gives it time to settle and soften, so it will look much better on the day.

✔ Do consider making an appointment at a male beauty salon.

Stag night

Stag nights traditionally celebrated the groom's last night of freedom and were held on the night before the wedding. (Don't even think about it!) Virtually all stag nights now happen at least a week before the wedding and often earlier. The emphasis has also shifted. They tend not just to be about embarrassing the groom so much as genuinely enjoying time with friends. They also tend to last for longer – a weekend is not unusual – and they often focus on an activity such as quad-biking, paint-balling or clay-pigeon shooting. Drinking, pranks and dubious jokes and stories from the best man still feature.

Stag nights are usually organised by the best man. It may be the first time for years that a group of old friends have been together, and it is important to find something that will appeal to everyone and make it an event to be remembered.

The best man should perhaps be gently reminded that he is supposed to look after the groom and make sure he gets home safely…

STAG NIGHT ORGANISATION

✓ Do find out when everyone is free.
✓ Do make an effort to invite old friends who may not live nearby.
✓ Do make sure everyone agrees to the plan and is committed.

✓ Do ask for a contribution towards costs or any deposit that must be paid.

Costs may include:
• Accommodation
• Travel
• Organising an activity break
• Food and drink
• Entertainment

Useful websites when planning a stag night include:
• **www.hitched.co.uk** which includes ideas for activities, suggestions, and offers 'props' to make sure the event is memorable in the Stag and Hen department in the **shop@hitched**.
• **www.exhilaration.co.uk** is the website for Extreme Sports (UK) Ltd and offers such attractions as air adventures, driving days, wet & wild, wine lovers, lazy days, group activities and parabounce.

The Weekend Company, tel: 0115 989 9889, organises city-based activity breaks in the UK.

In many ways, stag nights and hen parties are not dissimilar from each other, and it is no longer unusual for couples to hold a joint party with mutual friends if they prefer. The important thing is to do something that suits you.

COUNTDOWN TO THE CEREMONY

With everything organised, now is the time to confirm arrangements and make sure that all the preparations are going ahead as planned, all legalities have been attended to, all necessary documents have been obtained and everyone knows what they are doing.

Church weddings
MARRIAGE PREPARATION COURSE

There may be a set course of classes which engaged couples are asked to attend, or your minister may have set up a series of informal meetings to discuss the religious and emotional implications of marriage, the significance of the vows you are soon to take and some of the issues you will have to face in married life.

Some churches stipulate that you must attend. Others may be less strict, but the sessions are worthwhile and are intended to help your understanding of each other, the importance of the bond you are about to make and the church's views on marriage.

It is a good idea to take time out from the practicalities and concerns of organising a wedding to focus on what marriage is really all about.

REHEARSAL

This is a good opportunity for all the key people involved to get together – particularly the bride and groom, best man, chief bridesmaid and bridesmaids and parents. It is usually reassuring to run through the ceremony, check where everyone is supposed to stand and make sure you are familiar with the order of the service. For more information on wedding rehearsals, see page 30.

BANNS

Although it used to be considered bad luck for the bride and groom to hear their own banns being read out in church, it is now actively encouraged, and most couples make sure they attend church at least once during the three weeks when the banns are being announced. For more information on banns, see pages 28 and 55.

CEREMONY CONFIRMATIONS

✔ Do confirm your selections of hymns, music and readings.

✔ Do confirm final arrangements with the organist, choir and readers.

✔ Do speak to the flower arrangers at the church or the civil venue and check what flowers are available and their colours.

COUNTDOWN TO THE RECEPTION

As the replies to invitations begin to arrive, you should be chasing up guests who haven't yet answered and writing a final guest list.

RECEPTION ARRANGEMENTS CHECKLIST

Confirm numbers with the caterers ☐

Confirm guest list with the reception venue ☐

Confirm final arrangements with any suppliers – flowers, food, drink, musicians, DJs, fireworks, transport, etc. ☐

Seating plan ☐

As soon as you know guest numbers, finalise your seating plan ☐

SUPPLIERS CHECKLIST

Arrange a pre-wedding meeting with the photographer to confirm the number and exactly what photographs you want (have trial photos taken) ☐

Speak to the cake-maker to check there are no hitches and run through delivery details ☐

Speak to the florist and confirm your order. Discuss flowers that are available, colour scheme and final details ☐

Contact wedding transport companies – confirm the number and types of vehicles, any extras and times ☐

Take time out for both of you

If funds allow, try to get away for a weekend. Maybe someone you know has a cottage you could borrow for a couple of days so that you can spend time with each other and relax – walk by the sea or just enjoy fresh air and cosy pub lunches.

RELAXING PRE-WEDDING

✔ Do make time for each other.
✔ Do have fun.
✔ Do see friends.
✔ Do carry on with normal life and activities.
✔ Do remember why you are getting married in the first place.

Stress busters

Busy lives and too much work are often sufficient in themselves to make you feel stress. Fatigue, migraine, backache, stiff neck and poor digestion are just some of the symptoms. Planning a wedding, with the organisation involved and the extra things to remember, plus the strain of keeping everyone happy and smoothing over disputes between members of different families, can add considerably to stress levels in the months leading up to the big day.

There are various therapies and treatments available to help you beat stress and relax.

These include:

- Yoga
- Aromatherapy
- Aromatherapy massage
- Massage
- Shiatsu
- Reflexology
- Reiki
- Bach flower remedies

Other therapies and treatments are readily available, as well as a whole range of beauty treatments. Many weekend newspaper supplements carry regular features and articles appear in wedding magazines and other women's journals. GPs may be able to recommend alternative practitioners and telephone directories will list nearby health spas. It is also worth checking at good health stores.

Healthy diet and exercise

Eating a well-balanced, healthy diet, taking the time to eat slowly and digest, drinking plenty of water and getting enough rest are all important elements in combating stress and feeling great. Walking, swimming, working out at the gym, exercise classes and sport are all good ways of boosting energy levels and helping you to unwind and relax.

16 ON THE DAY

By the time the wedding day arrives, all the preparations should be complete and everyone involved should know exactly what they are supposed to be doing.

THE WEDDING MORNING

✓ Do arrange for someone to give you a wake-up call. This should be early enough to avoid rushing but not so early that you still feel tired.

✓ Do eat breakfast.

✓ Do have a long, hot bath – add some relaxing or stimulating essential oils depending on your mood.

✓ Do relax and enjoy your day.

Flowers

Your florist may be organising all the decorations, but if you are responsible for any, now is the time for them to be finished. Churches often allow flower arrangements inside the church only an hour or so before the ceremony.

Make any last-minute additions to the reception venue decorations if really necessary.

The best man should check that floral buttonholes and the order of service sheets have all been delivered to the church or other wedding venue.

Bouquets for the bride and bridesmaids should all be delivered to the bride.

Timetables

The following timetables are intended as a rough guide for how long you should allow for each stage. The specific times at which you will need to do everything will vary according to the time of the ceremony, how long the journey from home to the ceremony will take, how many pre-wedding photographs you are planning, just how elaborate your outfit and hairstyle are and how long you personally take. Depending on the time of day you are getting married, you may also need to allow for lunch.

Getting dressed on your wedding morning is the final stage of your preparations. The bride will be helped by her bridesmaids, mother and family, and the groom by his best man and family. The whole process should be as relaxed and as much fun as possible. Try to make time for a celebratory glass of something bubbly before you leave.

TIMETABLE FOR THE BRIDE

- After your bath, apply moisturiser.
- Depending on the style you have chosen, allow up to one and a half hours for your hair – you know best whether or not you should wash it on the wedding morning. Time how long it takes you to style your hair normally or, if you have booked a stylist, time how long your last practice appointment took.
- Allow up to an hour for make-up and an extra 10–15 minutes if you are applying nail polish.
- It will probably take 30–45 minutes to dress completely and arrange your headdress and veil.
- Allow about an hour for pre-wedding photographs.
- If you normally wear an engagement ring, move it to your right hand until after the wedding ceremony.

TIMETABLE FOR THE GROOM

- Bath, wash and style hair.
- Shave carefully and thoroughly – allow about 15 minutes.
- Polish shoes (if not polished the night before), which should take roughly 10 minutes.
- Dress in wedding clothes. This will probably take between 15 and 30 minutes.
- Unless you have made special arrangements, you will probably not be photographed until you arrive at church.
- Arrive early for the ceremony with your best man.

ON THE DAY CHECKLIST

Ask your best man, chief bridesmaid and parents to:

Make sure your honeymoon luggage is safely
stowed at your first-night hotel ☐

Look after your wedding clothes once you have
changed into your going-away outfits ☐

Return any hired clothes ☐

Take home wedding presents ☐

Send out wedding cake to guests unable to attend ☐

17 THE WEDDING CEREMONY

Church ceremonies

Ushers arrive first, ready to hand out buttonholes and order of service sheets, and to direct guests to their seats. The bride's family and friends sit on the left-hand side of the aisle and the groom's on the right. Parents sit in the front row and the closest relatives usually sit nearest the front.

Next to arrive are the minister, organist, choir and bell-ringers. The organist will start to play as guests are taking their places. Soon after the first guests and about 15 minutes before the service is due to begin, the groom and best man should arrive. The photographer will usually ask them to pose for pictures outside the church before going inside. The best man should check that the ushers have everything they need and give them any special instructions.

The groom and best man either wait in the vestry until the bride is due to arrive or stand or sit in the front pew to the right of the centre aisle. The groom sits on the best man's left.

The chief bridesmaid and the bride's other attendants and mother will usually arrive five to ten minutes before the ceremony. Most guests should be seated by now.

Last of all are the bride and her father. The bridesmaids and bride's mother arrange the bride's dress and veil and photographs will probably be taken. The chief usher leads the bride's mother to her seat in the front pew on the left-hand side. She reserves the space to her right, next to the aisle, for the bride's father.

It is seen as a sign that the ceremony is about to begin when the bride's mother has taken her place. The organist begins to play the chosen music for the procession.

THE PROCESSION

Sometimes the minister meets the bride at the church porch and returns with her to the altar, where the groom and best man are now standing to the right.

If there is a choir, they may lead the procession, followed by the minister, then the bride and her father, the chief bridesmaid and the other attendants walking in pairs, with the youngest in front.

The bride walks on her father's right, ready to take her place on the groom's left.

The groom and best man often turn towards the bride as she walks along the aisle. This should be the couple's first sight of one another on their wedding day.

KEY STAGES OF THE CEREMONY

20–30 minutes of music while guests are assembling

Music for the entrance of the bride and procession along the aisle

Minister's welcome and introduction

Opening hymn

The marriage ceremony, including the exchange of rings and vows

Second hymn*

Reading

Address or sermon

Any special readings and musical performances would be added here

Prayers

Blessing

Final hymn

Musical piece while the bridal party are signing the register

Music for the recessional while bride and groom, followed by the wedding party, walk back down the aisle and leave the church

*If only two hymns are wanted, it is usual to leave out the middle one and begin and end the ceremony with a hymn.

SIGNING THE REGISTER

The minister leads the bridal party, usually into the vestry, to sign the register and collect the marriage certificate. The procession order is minister, bride and groom, chief bridesmaid and best man, other attendants in pairs, bride's mother and groom's father, groom's mother and bride's father.

THE RECESSIONAL

This is the proper name for the procession out of the church. The order is the same as for the signing of the register, except the minister does not take part and the bride and groom lead. After the ceremony, there are photographs. The bride and groom leave first for the reception, closely followed by the bride's parents or whoever is acting as hosts. The best man and ushers make sure everyone has transport and no guests are stranded. The best man and bridesmaids share a car to the reception.

ROMAN CATHOLIC ORDER OF SERVICE

After the bride has joined the groom at the altar, the service starts with a hymn. There are Bible readings and a sermon which talks about the significance of marriage and the bond that is being made. There is a declaration that there is no lawful reason why the couple may not marry and the priest joins the couple's right hands. With the congregation as witnesses, the couple exchange vows, promising faithfulness and to bring up their children as Roman Catholics.

Once the priest has confirmed them in marriage, the best man hands him the ring or rings to bless. The groom also gives his bride gold and silver to represent his worldly possessions. When the ring is blessed the groom first places it on his bride's thumb, then on each of the next three fingers in turn, saying, 'In the name of the Father, the Son and the Holy Ghost, Amen.'

There are prayers and a blessing before the wedding party go into the sacristy to sign the register and make their civil marriage declaration.

The Nuptial Mass follows if there is to be one. After the final blessing and dismissal, the bride and groom lead the procession from the church.

Civil ceremonies

At a civil ceremony in a register office, the numbers of guests is often limited and you are discouraged from arriving too early. The wedding party and guests tend to arrive at much the same time, and the bride and groom may travel separately or together to the ceremony as they prefer. For civil weddings in other approved venues, the arrival arrangements may be much more like those at a traditional church wedding.

CEREMONY IN APPROVED PREMISES

When the superintendent registrar arrives, the couple will be spoken to in private to run through the exact procedure and check details. There will also be fees to be paid for the registrar's attendance and the marriage certificate.

The marriage room will be separate from other activities in the building and must remain open to the public. Guests will gather and the bride and groom will stand at the front, usually before a table where the registrars sit. The registrar will make a statement explaining the vows the couple are about to undertake. The bride and groom make their declaration that there is no legal reason why they should not be married and recite their vows. Rings may then be exchanged.

The marriage register must then be signed by the bride and groom, two witnesses and the registrar and superintendent registrar. The witnesses are usually the best man and the bride's father but they can be complete strangers.

REGISTER OFFICE CEREMONY

The superintendent registrar will attend your wedding, but it is usually the registrar who actually marries you. First the couple will be called for a private interview to check details, enter the marriage into the marriage notice book and complete the marriage certificate. Fees for the ceremony should also be paid.

The guests take their places in the wedding room and the couple and witnesses stand in front of the registrars. As with civil marriages in other licensed buildings, there is no religious content to the service, although you will probably be allowed to include readings from novels, poetry or songs. You should speak to your registrar to make sure he or she is happy with your selection.

The marriage statement and declaration are made, the couple exchange vows and rings, and the registrar pronounces them husband and wife. The marriage register is signed and witnessed.

Jewish weddings

Aside from the civil requirements, the first step is for couples to speak to the rabbi as there are various formalities which must be agreed. The rabbi will usually suggest further meetings to talk about marriage, your duties as husband and wife, and how to run a kosher home.

MIKVAH

In some Jewish ceremonies, the bride takes part in a *mikvah* ceremony or ritual washing at her synagogue a few days before the wedding. This is to purify her for marriage.

It is considered unlucky for Jewish couples to see each other for seven days before the wedding, although in practice most couples now stay apart for only one or two days, or a weekend.

THE WEDDING DAY

On the wedding morning, the couple fast and recite prayers. The bride usually wears a white or cream dress and a veil. Ceremonies vary in Orthodox and Reform synagogues, but men and women may sit in different parts of the synagogue and wear something on their heads. Jewish weddings can take place anywhere, and on any day except the Sabbath, which lasts from sunset on Friday until sunset on Saturday, but marriages are most often solemnised in a synagogue.

ORDER OF SERVICE

The groom arrives first with his father, best man and the bride's father. They are escorted to the front of the congregation and stand near the *chuppah*, which is a canopy supported by four poles. It is usually made from silk or velvet and decorated with flowers. There are various traditions and rituals which may be included.

Badeking This is the ritual unveiling of the bride, when the groom lifts back the veil from her face.

Chuppah The canopy represents the home the newlyweds will create and the divine presence beneath which they are married. The tradition remembers the time when the Jewish people were nomadic and lived in tents.

The bride and groom are escorted to the *chuppah* by their parents who carry candles to light their way. The bride stands on the right, and sometimes the couple's parents join them under the canopy, but everyone takes their positions as agreed with the rabbi beforehand.

The groom puts on a *kittel*, a white robe worn only on special days. Neither partner will wear any jewellery while under the *chuppah*, emphasising the importance of the ring the bride will receive.

The seven circles The bride circles the groom seven times, signifying that she is making him the centre of her life. The mothers of the couple follow, showing the two families will still be a part of the couple's new life together.

The nine blessings The first two are made over the glass of ritual wine and bless the betrothal.

The groom places the ring on his bride's right index finger and makes his wedding vows. The bride is not expected to reply and her silent acceptance of the ring is taken as her part of the marriage contract. The bride can then move the ring to the third finger of her left hand. After the *ketubah*, or marriage contract, is read aloud, seven more blessings are recited.

Breaking the glass The groom traditionally smashes to the ground the wine glass the couple have sipped from and crushes it under his heel. The glass is crushed to represent the Roman destruction of the Temple in Jerusalem.

Next the marriage covenant is signed and there is a further blessing and psalm of praise. The couple must then sign the synagogue register and civil contract.

Yichud Finally the bride and groom are allowed to be alone together for the first time for a short while. They may also break their fast.

Most rabbis are authorised to register marriages and so there is no need for a registrar to be present at the wedding.

Greek Orthodox weddings

There are sometimes several best men and women called *koumbari* and *kourneres*. The bride usually wears white and is met at the church door by a best man, who presents her with her bouquet of flowers.

The ceremony begins with the exchange of rings and culminates in the traditional crowning of the bride and groom with olive branches. It is a Greek custom that when a man makes his vows he must stamp his feet to show he will be 'in charge' in the marriage. Often today there is only the most subtle shifting of feet. To acknowledge the Holy Trinity, the couple kiss the Bible and walk three times around a table. Greek women wear their wedding rings on their right hand. The ring is actually worn on the left hand during the engagement and swapped at marriage.

At the reception there are Greek dances, including the money dance where guests pin notes and, less traditionally, cheques, to the couple's clothes as they dance. It is not unusual for couples to receive thousands of pounds to start their married life together.

Hindu weddings

Hindu weddings are steeped in ritual and custom. Some couples choose very traditional ceremonies that take several days while others prefer ones lasting only a few hours. Hindu weddings are much more a community gathering than a simple family affair. Not all weddings are alike and it is impossible to give anything more than a general idea.

Current Hindu wedding ceremonies have evolved over many thousands of years and consist of a core of rituals considered essential in the Vedas, the ancient Hindu scriptures. Some couples opt for all the traditional rituals, others only for those which have special meaning for them.

When a couple have decided to marry, traditionally both families will visit a priest, who will study their horoscopes and find an auspicious day for the wedding. Next is the *thaka* which is really where the marriage is announced. The dowry is now symbolic and the bride's family visit the groom's family to give them sweets and pastries as a symbol of happiness.

THE BRIDE

A few days before the wedding, the bride's female relatives and friends hold a *sangeet* where they sing traditional wedding songs to the bride.

The night before, there are three ceremonies.

The first is the *choora*, when the bride's uncle places red bangles on her wrist. These are to show she is no longer single and she will wear the bangles for about a week after the wedding. The second ceremony is for purification, involving *hakhi* or turmeric. The bride is then given a *kangan* which is a bracelet including such things as a ring, seashells and beads. This is slipped on to her wrist by a *pandit* or priest. The third ceremony is called *mendhi ki raat*. The bride's (and those of some of her female friends) hands, feet and arms are decorated with henna. This is said to ensure your mother-in-law will love you, and the darker the henna, the better you will get along.

THE GROOM

A female relation, usually accompanied by other relatives, fetches water from the nearest temple in a clay pot which is then poured over the groom's head to purify him. This ceremony is known as *ghadoli* and takes place the day before the wedding.

The night before, the groom has his own *mendhi* ceremony where he puts henna handprints on to a wall in his home. A *pandit* then places a *kangan* on his wrist just like the bride's.

Traditionally, that night the groom goes to sleep away from home, pretending to be angry with his family. They find him and bring him home.

THE WEDDING CEREMONY

On the day, the bride is dressed in red and her traditional sari perhaps richly embroidered with gold and silver thread. Her lavish robes are complemented by family jewellery. The groom is usually dressed in white or ivory.

The morning of the wedding is when the engagement takes place. There is a ring ceremony and an exchange of gifts. Everyone has lunch and the groom's family leave.

In the evening everyone dresses up and the groom's party go to the *sehra bundi*, where the groom has a turban and crown placed on his head. Relatives hang garlands of flowers and money around his neck. This begins the *baraat*, or procession, of the groom, his family and his friends to the wedding, where the bride is already waiting.

The bride's family meet the groom's at the entrance and they exchange flower garlands. The bride's family will already have set up a *mandap*, or canopy, supported by four pillars which represent the four parents. The bride's brothers and uncles accompany the groom to his seat beneath the *mandap*.

The bride is brought out by her brothers from where she is hiding to join the groom. The couple then exchange flower garlands. A fire is started under the *mandap* and offerings of rice, oils, ghee and flowers are thrown into the flames. Prayers or mantras are recited and the bride's and groom's hands may be joined, which is called *hastamelaap*.

Circling the fire The bride and groom circle the fire four times and four blessings are given, for wealth, good health, happiness and prosperity. The four circles around the fire signify religion (*dharma*), wealth (*artha*), family/children (*kaam*) and salvation (*moksha*).

Seven steps towards happiness The couple then take seven steps together. This is a traditional ritual known as *saptapadi*. The seven steps symbolise ideals, strength and power, health and fortune, happiness, children, long life and spiritual friendship. Sometimes the bride will step on a stone to signify her faithfulness and loyalty to the marriage.

Wedding vows and blessing The bride and groom may make more offerings of rice and food to the fire. Sometimes the couple are sprinkled with puffed rice for prosperity and flower petals after they exchange vows, and the bride may be given a *mangal sutra*, or symbolic necklace, when rings are exchanged.

Often the groom will make a marriage mark on his new bride's forehead with *sedhu*, or an orange powder, to show she is now married. The couple then touch each of the four parents' feet and receive their blessings. Afterwards there is a lavish wedding feast.

For more information, check:
• **www.ehow.com** (specifically eHow to Plan a Hindu Wedding)

Muslim weddings

The Muslim wedding ceremony is called a *nikah* and it is a civil contract. It may consist of no more than a simple declaration and acceptance in front of two male witnesses. The exact form is very much up to the *qazi*, the person who performs the wedding.

On the day of the *nikah*, men and women remain in separate rooms. Only the men hear the marriage contract. Usually the *qazi*, the groom and the bride's father, plus two male witnesses, meet to agree the amount of dowry the groom will give.

Following a short ceremony, in which passages may be read from the first chapter of the Koran, the bride's father and two witnesses go to the women's room to ask the bride if she will accept the groom as her husband. Often the groom is then taken to the women's room, where he stands at the doorway. He gives money and gifts to the bride's sister and is blessed by the older women. He returns to the men's hall and both rooms start their own separate receptions, which are called *valimas*. There is usually food, music and dancing.

Afterwards the couple may sit together for the first time and a *dupatta* covers their heads while prayers are said. Sweets or dates are sometimes given out to guests, and the elders often give money to children.

18 MUSIC, READINGS & SPEECHES

Music and words are an essential part of any wedding – at both the ceremony and the reception. They can reflect your feelings for one another and make the occasion much more personal and intimate for both you and your families.

Music is a vital element for most people and adds considerably to the joy and excitement of the celebration. Readings can have special significance and speeches are an opportunity for others to toast the newlyweds and lighten the tone, marking the end of the formalities and the start of the more informal part of the day.

Only you can decide exactly what music you want to hear as you walk up the aisle. Only you can decide what texts might be read during your wedding ceremony. Only you can decide whom you want to deliver speeches at your wedding reception. Others will certainly have opinions and those close to you are worth listening to when they offer the wisdom of experience. Family politics can involve compromise, however, so be prepared to give ground on certain issues if you have to in order to make sure that whatever is most important to you goes the way you want.

MUSIC FOR RELIGIOUS WEDDINGS

Roman Catholic and Baptist churches will allow only religious music to be played, while the Society of Friends do not include music of any kind in their wedding ceremonies.

The church minister is responsible, not only for the worship but also for the music played in his church, so you should discuss your choices with him or her beforehand. The organist or choir master will also be able to help and give you some idea of their abilities – it would be pointless to choose a beautiful but exceptionally tricky piece if the organist was unable to play it well.

Music in church

Organ music is the most usual accompaniment to church weddings. Most churches have organs and the sound is rich and powerful enough to fill the space. It is possible to include solo instruments, groups of musicians or singers in your ceremony, but you should always speak to the minister and, as a courtesy, to the organist first. You could also play CDs or other recordings but these are often not so effective.

It is usual for the organist to begin playing while the guests are taking their places before the arrival of the bride. You may ask for specific pieces to be played or you can leave the choice to the organist. The bride and groom normally decide on the music to be played at the arrival of the bride. The other key points when music is played are during the signing of the register and the recessional, when the newlywed couple and the bridal party process back down the aisle and leave the church.

You may already have firm favourites which you would like to hear at your wedding. If not, the vicar and organist can make suggestions and there are CDs and cassettes of wedding music which you could listen to before making your final selection.

Wedding music
Favourites (as listed by the organ master at a popular London church):

AT THE BRIDE'S ENTRANCE
Charpentier *Trumpet Tune* (or *Prelude to Te Deum*)
Jeremiah Clarke *Trumpet Voluntary*
Pachelbel *Canon* (if couples want the American favourite 'weepy' entrance, rather than the traditional English rousing one)
Purcell *Trumpet Tune and Air*

AS THE BRIDAL PARTY LEAVES
Handel *Arrival of the Queen of Sheba* (although the name suggests otherwise, it works better for going

out than arriving because it is quite long)
Handel 'Hornpipe' (from *Water Music*)
Mendelssohn 'Wedding March' (from *A Midsummer Night's Dream*)
Widor *Toccata*

Other popular choices

AS GUESTS ARE ARRIVING

Bach 'Sheep May Safely Graze', or extracts from Brandenburg Concertos No. 3 and No. 4; Brahms theme from the *St Anthony Chorale*; Elgar 'Nimrod' from the *Enigma Variations*; Handel Hornpipe in F, Coro, Minuet No. 2 extracts from Organ Concerto No. 6; Parry *Bridal March*.

AT THE ENTRANCE OF THE BRIDE (OR PROCESSIONAL)

Beethoven Hallelujah Chorus (from *The Mount of Olives*); Bliss 'A Wedding Fanfare'; Bride 'Allegro Marzialle'; Mozart Wedding March (from *The Marriage of Figaro*); Purcell 'Fanfare'; Saint-Saëns Opening of the Fourth Movement from Symphony No. 3; Verdi Grand March from *Aida*; Wagner Bridal Chorus from *Lohengrin* ('Here comes the bride' – this is now rarely chosen)

CHORAL AND ORGAN PIECES

To be played during the signing of the register and at other points in the service.

Albinoni Adagio in G Minor; Bach Air on a G String; Byrd 'Sing Joyfully'; Dowland 'Come Again, Sweet Love Doth Now Invite'; Handel 'Air' from *Water Music*; Howells 'Behold O God Our Defender', Psalm 121 from the Requiem; Monteverdi 'Beatus Vir'; Mozart Romanze (from *Eine Kleine Nachtmusik*), Exsultate Jubilate (for a soprano soloist); Palestrina Sanctus and Agnus Dei (from *Missa Brevis*); Rutter 'Toccata in Seven'; Vaughan Williams Chorale Prelude on Rhosymedre; Vivaldi Laudamus te (from *Gloria*, for two soprano soloists); Walton 'Set Me as a Seal Upon Thy Heart'

RECESSIONAL
(as the bride and groom leave): Elgar 'Pomp and Circumstance' March No. 4; Hollins Bridal March; Mendelssohn 'Carillon-Sortie'; Purcell Wedding March; Kargellert 'Now Thank We All Our God'; Vierne Finale from Symphony No.1; Walton *Crown Imperial*; Whitlock 'Fanfare'

CHOIR PIECES FOR AN AMATEUR CHOIR
Bach 'Jesu Joy of Man's Desiring'
Wesley 'Love one Another'

CHOIR PIECES FOR A MORE ADVANCED CHOIR
Fauré *Cantique de Jean Racine*
Hadley 'My Beloved Spake'
Parry 'I was Glad'
Vivaldi *Gloria*

SOLOIST PIECES
Bach 'Ave Maria'
Gounod 'Ave Maria'
Handel 'Let the Bright Seraphim'
Handel 'He shall feed His Flock' (from *The Messiah*)
Mozart 'Laudate Dominum'
Schubert 'Ave Maria'

Hymns

Two or three hymns are generally sung at church weddings. The first one after the minister's introduction is usually in praise of God and the second, after the marriage vows, is a celebration of love. However, there are no fixed rules. It is worth thinking about the length of some hymns and, especially if there is no choir to help the congregation, it may be a good idea to omit one or two verses. Any verses which are not appropriate for weddings can also be left out.

If you are reproducing the words for hymns on your order of service sheets always check for copyright holders listed in hymn and other books. Always contact the copyright holder – they may ask for a small fee or an acknowledgement.

POPULAR WEDDING HYMNS
All creatures of our God and King
All my hope on God is founded

All People that on earth do dwell
All things bright and beautiful
Alleluya! Sing to Jesus
And did those feet in ancient time (Jerusalem)
At the name of Jesus
Come down O Love divine
Dear Lord and Father of mankind
Father, hear the prayer we offer
For the beauty of the earth
Give me joy in my heart
God of all living
Guide me, oh Thou great Redeemer
Happy are they, they that love God
How great Thou art
Immortal, invisible, God only wise
I vow to Thee my Country
Jesus, good above all other
Jesus stands among us
Lead us, heavenly Father, lead us
Lord of all hopefulness
Lord of the dance
Love divine, all loves excelling
Make me a channel of Thy peace
Morning has broken
Now thank we all our God
O God, whose loving hand has led
O Holy Spirit, Lord of grace
O Jesus I have promised

O perfect Love, all human thought transcending
O Praise ye the Lord!
One more step along the
world I go
Praise to the Lord, the Almighty, the King of Creation
Praise, my soul, the King of heaven
Sing praise to the Lord!
Take my life and let it be
Tell out my soul, the Greatness of the Lord
The King of Love my shepherd is
The Lord's my Shepherd
Thine for ever! God of love

Musicians

Check the classified advertisements at the back of
bride magazines for musicians, CDs and musical
coordinators. Alternatively, you could contact local
operatic societies, music conservatories or the music
departments of universities and colleges.

Bells

Many churches no longer have bells or bell-ringers.
If your church does, you may want a glorious peal of
bells to welcome you to the service, and afterwards
to announce and celebrate your marriage. Fees vary
according to how many bells and bell-ringers there
are – very large churches will have eight bells,
though six is more usual and occasionally four,

and the charges will be around £10 to £30 per bell. You should make sure bell-ringers are available when you book your wedding day.

Organist and choir

Always arrange in advance if you want an organist and choir at your wedding. There will be a fee for the church organist and choir, and some churches ask for extra donations – for the upkeep of the organ, for instance. If your chosen church does not have a choir, you could employ a quartet of professional choral singers. This has certain advantages – since they are professionals they will be able to sing anything and will give a good lead for the congregation in the hymn singing. Any extra expense for organist and choir is probably worth paying, in return for the better quality of music.

Equity and the Musicians' Union stipulate that fees should be doubled if a service is to be recorded. Some places are stricter about this than others and many will only add on a percentage – if the usual fee for the organist is £80 this will be raised to £100 and £75 for a singer instead of £50.

If you are planning on a video recording of the ceremony, you should tell the organist or musical director as this may affect costs because recording or copyright fees may have to be charged.

Here is a rough guide to costs:

Organist £35–£100 (rates tend to be higher in London)

Parish church choir £120–£150

Professional choral singers £50 each

Music for civil weddings

The choice of music is entirely up to you, although it should be non-religious. You should tell the registrar your choices and check that the facilities for playing music are adequate. If you want to hire musicians to play, you should make sure they are appropriate for the size of the venue.

READINGS

It is possible to leave the choice of readings to the minister and most will be very happy to offer advice. Or it may be that there are particular biblical passages or psalms which have a special meaning for you, and which you would like to include in your wedding ceremony.

There must be one reading from Scripture, but certainly in the Anglican Church couples often choose extracts from Shakespeare, Plato, John Donne and even Byron. The rule, as always, is to check with your minister. Most will be glad to include readings which make the ceremony more personal, as long as they are suitable, and you should also ask if you wish a close friend or family member to read or to conduct any of the prayers.

The Bible

For possible wedding readings, look at the following psalms:

• Psalm 23 'The Lord is my shepherd'
• Psalm 37 'Put thou thy trust in the Lord'
• Psalm 84 'How lovely is your dwelling-place'
• Psalm 128 'Blessed are all they that fear the Lord and walk in his ways'
• Psalm 139 'O Lord you have searched me'

For the creation story, look at:

• Genesis 1:27–31
• Genesis 2:18–24

Proverbs and the Song of Songs are good sources of inspiration. Two particularly popular readings are 'Two are better than one', Ecclesiastes 4:9–12, and the wedding at Cana, John 2:1–11.

On the importance and qualities of love, look at the following:

• 1 Corinthians 13:1–13
• 1 John 4:7–12
• John 15:9–12
• Ephesians 3:14–19
• Ephesians 5:21–33
• Romans 12:1,2,9–13
• Colossians 3:12–17

Other possible readings

A copy of *The Oxford Dictionary of Quotations* is a good starting point when searching for readings. You can look up subjects such as Love or Marriage in the index and find references for quotes which may lead you on to longer passages. You can check specific authors and there are also biblical quotations.

Authors to check more thoroughly include:

• William Shakespeare – sonnets and plays
• Bishop Jeremy Taylor – *Sermons. The Marriage Ring*
• Elizabeth Barrett Browning – letters and poems, including 'How do I love thee?'
• John Donne – including 'Come live with me, and be my love'
• Lord Byron – including 'She walks in beauty, like the night'

Plus a whole host of modern authors and poets.

Useful reading:
The Oxford Dictionary of Quotations
Weddings – Prayers, Hymns and Readings to Help You Plan the Day by Andrew Best and Jackie Hunt

Useful websites:
• **www.hitched.co.uk**
• **www.wedding-service.co.uk**
• **www.qm4.com**

WEDDING SPEECHES

The speeches and toasts take place at the end of the meal, usually before the cutting of the wedding cake. The purpose is really to congratulate the newlyweds and wish them happiness in their future life together, and also to thank various people.

Increasingly, brides are choosing to make a speech at their own wedding, or to ask their chief bridesmaid to speak on their behalf, and this is now considered perfectly acceptable and not unusual, although there is no compulsion to speak if the idea horrifies.

The time for speeches can be a moment of dread for many best men and fathers, but there is no reason why even the most inexperienced public speaker cannot make a good speech. At least at a wedding everyone is usually in a good mood – well fed, cheered by champagne and wine, and wanting to join in wishing the married couple well.

SPEECHES

✓ Do remember that the speeches are not the most vital part of the wedding and if all you can muster are a few words of thanks and a toast to the newlyweds, no one will mind.

✓ Do prepare. No one but the most gifted and accomplished speaker can deliver a speech without preparation.

✗ Don't speak for too long. The best speeches are often the shortest.

Ways to present a speech

Write your speech and then read it aloud The disadvantage to this is that it lacks spontaneity and does not allow for any amusing incidents from the day to be added.

Memorise the speech Very few people can manage this successfully, especially when nervous.

Use card notes with key words or phrases These prompt your thoughts, make sure you cover everything and allow you flexibility to shorten or add as seems appropriate on the day.

Witty speeches

It is often a good idea to include a funny anecdote or joke in a wedding speech and you may be able to think of the perfect story.

JOKES IN SPEECHES

✔ Do remember your audience. A joke or story that the groom would find funny with his mates in the pub may not be a good idea with family and elderly relations at a wedding.

✔ Don't make jokes at the expense of the bride (or her mother) or ones they would find particularly offensive.

A best man who has known the groom for a long time could refer to key events in the groom's life, and can make jokes at the groom's expense, as long as they are basically affectionate and not offensive to anyone else.

A safer alternative to jokes may be to use one or two well-chosen quotations – more than that could sound pompous. Writers like Oscar Wilde, George Bernard Shaw and Dorothy Parker, performers such as Groucho Marx and Mae West, and historical figures from Socrates to Catherine the Great and Samuel Johnson are all good sources.

'I require only three things of a man. He must be handsome, ruthless and stupid' – Dorothy Parker

'Marriage has many pains, but celibacy has no pleasures' – Samuel Johnson

'A man is in general better pleased when he has a good dinner upon his table than when his wife talks Greek' – Samuel Johnson

'Marriage…hath in it less of Beauty, but more of safety than the Single Life; it hath more Care, but less Danger; it is more Merry, and more Sad; is fuller of Sorrows, and fuller of Joys; it lies under more Burdens, but is supported by all the Strengths of Love and Charity, and those Burdens are delightful' – Bishop Jeremy Taylor

'Marriage is popular because it combines the maximum of temptation with the maximum of opportunity' – George Bernard Shaw

Many of the best wedding websites offer guidelines for speeches. Try:

- **www.hitched.co.uk**
- **www.confetti.co.uk**

SPEECHES

✓ Do practise out loud and in front of a mirror beforehand.

✓ Do try recording yourself – you may be surprised by how many times you repeat certain phrases or words.

✓ Do relax and try to appear confident.

✓ Do try to look just above the guests' heads.

✓ Do look at the people you are toasting.

✓ Do smile.

Do take a few deep breaths before you start.

Do have a glass of water to hand.

Do decide in advance what you are going to do with your hands.

✓ Do speak clearly and loudly without shouting.

✗ Don't stare – try to look natural.

✗ Don't try to speak until the audience is quiet.

✗ Don't look up at the ceiling or down at the floor.

✗ Don't drink too much alcohol before your speech – it won't help.

✗ Don't wave your arms around wildly or fiddle.
✗ Don't use a microphone unless you are used to speaking into one.
✗ Don't speak too quickly. Remember to breathe and pause.

Order of speeches
Toastmaster
Bride's father
Bridegroom
Best man

The toastmaster or best man should make a brief announcement for each speaker and call for quiet.

The first speech and toast
These are now usually made by the bride's father or the person who has given the bride away, although in the past the first speech was made by someone from the bride's party, a close male relative or family friend.

The speaker should begin by talking about the bride, possibly about her growing up, and should always be positive and praising. He should welcome the groom and his parents into the family. The speech should continue with a few words about the couple and end with a toast to the bride and groom or 'the happy couple'.

The second speech

This is made by the groom, replying to the first speech on behalf of his new wife and himself. He should thank the speaker for his toast and say how happy he is to be joining his wife's family.

The groom's speech is very much a list of thank-yous – to the bride's parents (or the wedding hosts) for the wonderful wedding (adapted if his parents have contributed or if he and the bride have paid for all or part of the wedding), to his own parents, to the guests and anyone who has been particularly helpful, to the bridesmaids for looking so delightful and for all their assistance, to his best man and ushers.

He should present any gifts at this point and he may wish to say something about, or to, his new wife.

The groom may also wish to respond to something particular in the first speech or to reflect on the day so far. He ends with a toast to the bridesmaids.

If the bride or chief bridesmaid are to make a speech, this is the point at which it should be delivered. What is said is entirely up to the bride. There are no conventions governing what is included.

As this speech intervenes between the toast to the bridesmaids and the best man's reply, it is a good idea to discuss the order of speeches and toasts with the best man in advance.

The final speech

This is made by the best man. He will reply to the toast on behalf of the bridesmaids by thanking the groom, and often adds a few compliments of his own. He will also thank anyone who has specifically helped him with his duties, and may thank someone on behalf of the bride.

The best man's speech is traditionally the main speech. It is usually lighter in tone than the others and more humorous.

The best man should congratulate the bride and groom and may repeat some suitable anecdotes about them, or more particularly about the groom.

He will end by proposing a toast to absent friends, if appropriate, and finally to the bride and groom.

He concludes by reading telemessages or cards from guests unable to attend the wedding, then announces the cutting of the cake and any programme for the remainder of the reception.

THE BEST MAN'S SPEECH

Thanks on behalf of the bridesmaids.

Compliments to the bridesmaids.

Congratulations to the happy couple.

Stories about the groom.

Toast to the host and hostess and to absent friends.

Toast to the bride and groom's future happiness.

Read out any telegrams or special messages.

Announce the cake-cutting and agenda for the rest of the proceedings.

19 THE HONEYMOON

A honeymoon should be more than just another holiday. It marks the start of your married life and should be special – somewhere you have dreamed of visiting for years or that you want to see together. After all the hard work and excitement of a wedding, it is an opportunity for you to spend time alone to celebrate and enjoy.

Deciding on a destination

The first thing you need to do is decide the type of honeymoon you both want, including the destination and the budget. Would you prefer to lie on a beach, take a cultural trip, go for misty moorland walks, find your own slice of paradise on a tropical island or go trekking in the Himalayas? For inspiration, look in bride magazines, on wedding websites and ask friends for recommendations.

There are a vast range of specialist tours and luxury packages to choose from, and many companies will tailor-make an itinerary to suit you if you can't find what you are looking for in a brochure. One popular option is to book a two-centre honeymoon, starting with a relaxed beach or countryside location and then moving on to a city or a safari.

More couples than ever are choosing to spend their honeymoon in the UK and it is worth calling the local tourist board about any area that particularly interests you to ask for recommendations. If you feel that a week's break is beyond your budget, think about staying somewhere luxurious for a romantic long weekend.

Traditionally, it was always the groom who chose and paid for the honeymoon, and although today most couples share the expense, some grooms still like to make the honeymoon a surprise. If you are planning this, do make sure it is something your fiancée will enjoy and give her advice about what to pack.

RECOMMENDED TRAVEL BOOKS

100 Best Romantic Resorts of the World by Katherine Dyson (Globe Pequot Press, 2000, £15.99)

Hip Hotels by Herbert Ypma (Thames & Hudson, 1999, £18.95)

Checklist for a Perfect Honeymoon by Suzanne Rodrigues-Hunter (Doubleday Books, 1996, £5.95)

Michelin Guides are good sources for hotels and restaurants.

With their many pictures, *Dorling Kindersley Eyewitness Travel Guides* give a good idea of what a country or city is like, and also contain addresses for hotels and restaurants in a variety of price ranges.

CHOOSING A HONEYMOON

✔ Do try to pick somewhere different that neither of you has visited before.

✔ Do choose a reputable company.

✔ Do look at a range of destinations and packages.

✔ Do compare quality, price and value for money.

✔ Do tell the hotel, airline, tour operator or travel agent that it is your honeymoon – there are often special extras for honeymooners and a better chance of an upgrade.

✔ Do arrange a few surprises for your partner, especially if you have planned everything together.

✘ Don't risk a disaster with your honeymoon by taking a chance on a dodgy deal.

✘ Don't choose somewhere either of you stayed with an ex-lover.

Hip honeymoon destinations

Recent trends include romantic honeymoons in Irish and Scottish castles, chic city hotels in London and New York, idyllic Caribbean islands, historic houses in France and Italy, Spanish sunshine and sea, travel to the exotic eastern bazaars of Morocco and India, and the best of all worlds with two-centre stays combining city and sun.

Vaccinations

Check whether your honeymoon destination requires you to have any inoculations and whether it

is advisable to begin taking malaria tablets. Your GP
should be able to answer any queries.

BEFORE TRAVELLING

✔ Do plan ahead if you are changing your name. You can
travel in your old single name, but you should book the
airline ticket in the same name as your passport or take
your marriage certificate.

✔ Do make sure your passports are up to date and if
needed apply for a visa at least a month before
travelling.

✔ Do make sure you have had all the necessary
vaccinations well before the wedding.

✔ Do apply for an international driving licence if needed.

✔ Do allow sufficient time for travel, especially getting to
and from airports.

✗ Don't forget to confirm tickets and reservations.

✗ Don't forget to organise foreign currency.

✗ Don't forget travel insurance if you are honeymooning
abroad.

✗ Don't make travel arrangements too complex.

Documents

At the wedding, the best man should take charge of
all travel documents – passports, visas, tickets and
any holiday currency or traveller's cheques, and make
sure they are safe.

Don't forget to collect them from him when you leave the reception, and give yourself sufficient travel time to get to your destination.

Passports

If you are changing your surname upon marriage and want to travel under your new married name, it is possible to change the name on your passport before the wedding. You must ask a registered church minister or registrar to sign the relevant form and then return it to the passport office with your passport. Ideally, allow at least one month for this, and longer during spring and summer months.

It may be easier to have any tickets issued in your maiden name and take along your marriage certificate in case of confusion.

Travel insurance

When deciding on a travel agent or tour operator, it is important to choose a reputable firm and a member of ABTA. This means the company will be fully insured should anything go wrong.

You should take out your own personal travel insurance to cover accident, illness, theft and travel delay. Your travel agent will be able to advise, or contact your usual company.

For online travel insurance:
* **www.travelinsuranceclub.co.uk**

USEFUL HONEYMOON WEBSITES

* **www.honeymoons.com** (an American site good
  for information about destinations and ideas)
* **www.justhoneymoons.net**
* **www.kuoni.co.uk**, or tel: 01306 747007
* **www.britishairwaysholidays.co.uk**,
  or tel: 0845 606 0747
* **www.sandals.com**
* **www.thomascook.com**
* **www.its.net** (general travel service)
* **www.lastminute.com** (hotels, holidays, London
  restaurants and entertainment)
* **www.vtourist.com**.
  (the virtual tourist: this includes recommendations
  and tips and allows you to explore destinations)
* **www.travel-library.com**
  (recommendations and hard facts)
* **www.fco.gov.uk/travel** (general advice from the
  Foreign Office; also information about safety and visas)
* **www.visitbritain.com** (British Tourist Authority)
* **www.informationbritain.co.uk**
* **www.cheapflights.co.uk** (for cheap flights)

The first night

Not surprisingly, there are various superstitions about a couple's first wedded night together. In Ireland, it was common practice to tie a hen to the bedpost and in Scotland a lactating woman made up the marriage bed. Both of these customs were to encourage fertility.

Until Victorian times it was quite usual for the bride and groom to be accompanied publicly to bed. One custom had bridesmaids and groomsmen standing on each side of the bed. They then threw the newly married couple's stockings over their shoulders, and if one of the girls hit the groom or one of the men hit the bride, this signified they would be the next to marry. The modern version of this tradition is the bride throwing her bouquet. Just as in the past, whoever catches the flowers will supposedly soon marry.

There is something symbolic about the first night together as a married couple. And however long you may have lived together already, there is an excitement about escaping from the attention and bustle of the wedding to spend time alone.

Try to plan your honeymoon proper to start the day after your wedding and avoid spending your first night in an airport lounge or travelling. If your reception is held in a hotel, you may be offered a complimentary room, though you may opt for the privacy of leaving guests behind and staying elsewhere.

It is a good idea to choose somewhere not too far from the reception, and remember to let them know you are newlyweds. It is not unusual for hotels to surprise honeymooners with champagne, chocolates or an extra-special room.

If you decide to stay in your own home, add to the romance with flowers, candles and champagne on ice. Whether at home or away, organise a delicious breakfast with all your favourite foods. Unless you are rushing off to catch a plane, plan to do something together – take advantage of the facilities on offer at your hotel, go for a leisurely country walk, take a boat trip, eat lunch at your favourite restaurant or whatever you particularly enjoy. Just generally spoil yourselves.

Don't forget to arrange transport to the airport if you are flying away on honeymoon.

Useful websites for hotels in the UK:
- **www.a2btravel.co.uk**
- **www.laterooms.co.uk**
- **www.londontown.com**
- **www.lastminute.com**

Budget savers

While not wanting to stint on your honeymoon, there are ways to cut costs and still have a really special holiday.

- You will probably save money on travel by honeymooning in the UK.
- Take your own car across the Channel. Especially away from high summer, there are many good deals to be had, both from ferry companies and from the Channel Tunnel operators. Hotels and restaurants in France are often good value.
- Some tour operators offer discounts to newlyweds, so shop around.
- By booking early, you may be in line to snap up special offers.
- Conversely, by leaving your booking to the last minute, you can also make savings, although your choice may be restricted.

HONEYMOON CHECKLIST

Holiday booked from work (dates)	❑
Departure time from reception	❑
Transport arranged from reception	❑
First night accommodation booked	❑
First night address	❑
Telephone/email/fax	❑

Honeymoon destination ☐
Honeymoon dates ☐
Travel agent's address ☐
Honeymoon accommodation address ☐
Essential documents:
    Passports ☐
    Visas ☐
    Marriage certificate ☐
    Tickets (plane, train, boat) ☐
    Driving licences ☐
Credit cards and UK money ☐
Foreign currency ☐
Vaccinations (if needed) ☐
Maps ☐
Guidebooks ☐
Timetables ☐
Return journey ☐

When you return from honeymoon
THANK YOUS
However organised you were before the wedding, extra gifts are sure to have arrived on the day, and you should try to send handwritten thank-you notes for these as soon as possible.

The bride's mother should also thank everyone who helped her with the preparations and on the day.

Guests should write a short note to the bride's parents or hosts thanking them.

DINNER

It is traditional for the newlywed couple to invite both sets of parents, followed by the best man, bridesmaids and ushers, to their new home, usually for a meal, in the first few months after the wedding.

You may also wish to invite those guests who were unable to attend on the day.

APPENDICES

WEDDING PLANNER

One of the simplest ways to solve the problem of too many things to remember is to make a list. Here you will find seven checklists to help you organise your time and know exactly what you should be doing when.

SIX MONTHS BEFORE THE WEDDING (OR AS SOON AS POSSIBLE)

Confirm the wedding date with the minister or registrar ☐

With the ceremony confirmed, confirm the reception ☐

Work out a guest list – agree it with both families ☐

Confirm your booking with the caterers. Discuss and agree a menu and drinks for the reception ☐

Book a photographer, and videographer if you're having one ☐

Organise a florist and discuss decorations, bouquets and buttonholes ☐

If necessary, also speak to the flower arranger at the church or other wedding venue ☐

Order your wedding dress ☐

Choose bridesmaids' and other attendants clothes ☐

Decide on the groom's wedding clothes ❏

Decide attire for best man, ushers and fathers ❏

Consider honeymoon options and book early ❏

Choose and order wedding invitations and wedding stationery (excluding order of service sheets) ❏

Order wedding cake ❏

THREE MONTHS BEFORE THE WEDDING

Arrange another meeting with the minister to discuss service, readings and music ❏

Book musicians ❏

Organise any other entertainment ❏

For a civil wedding, organise meeting with the superintendent registrar and book registrar and ceremony. Discuss choice of music and readings ❏

Organise wedding-dress fittings, buy wedding accessories (veil, headdress, etc.) and shoes ❏

Find a hairstylist and discuss wedding hairstyles ❏

Finalise details of groom's and attendants' wedding outfits ❏

Choose wedding rings ❏

Book wedding transport ❏

Draw up a wedding-gift list and place at the store or with the company of your choice ❏

Check your household insurance policy and
consider taking out wedding insurance ☐

Finalise honeymoon plans ☐

Book your wedding-night room if you are
planning on staying in a hotel ☐

Check that your passports are valid. If you are
changing your name, send off your passport
and name-change form ☐

Arrange vaccinations and visas if needed ☐

TWO MONTHS BEFORE

Send out invitations (no less than six weeks
before the wedding and no more than twelve) ☐

Keep a note of invitation replies ☐

Send gift-list information and thank-you notes
when gifts arrive. Keep a list of the presents ☐

Finalise the order of service and order printed sheets ☐

Choose your going-away and honeymoon clothes ☐

Choose presents for the bridesmaids, best man,
ushers, parents and anyone you wish to thank ☐

If you are changing your name, inform banks, etc. ☐

Reconfirm in writing all bookings – ceremony,
reception, caterers, photography, florist, musicians, etc. ☐

ONE MONTH TO GO

Chase up late replies to invitations ❑

Write a final guest list and confirm numbers
with reception venue and caterers ❑

Work out a seating plan ❑

Confirm transport arrangements ❑

Pay registrar for marriage certificate ❑

Visit hairdresser with headdress, finalise hairstyle,
arrange final appointment and/or book hairdresser
for wedding morning ❑

Book wedding make-up session ❑

Wear in wedding shoes at home ❑

Organise stag night and hen party ❑

Order holiday currency ❑

TWO WEEKS TO GO

Final haircuts should not be left any closer to the day ❑

Make a final, detailed check on complete
wedding outfits ❑

ONE WEEK TO GO

Arrange wedding rehearsal ❑

Reconfirm all arrangements – reception, flowers,
photographer, musicians, transport, entertainment, etc. ❑

Check that groom, father and best man are
writing speeches ☐

Bride should write her own speech if she is giving one ☐

Practise wedding hair and make-up ☐

Pack for honeymoon ☐

Sort out all necessary documents and keep
them in a safe place ☐

THE DAY BEFORE

Help decorate reception venue ☐

Ensure wedding cake is delivered safely ☐

Make sure all wedding clothes are ready ☐

Have a manicure ☐

If possible, relax – have a massage and sleep well ☐

MARRIED FINANCES

One of the major causes of disagreements between couples is money and it is important to sit down and consider the financial and legal implications of marriage calmly.

A joint bank account?

Most banks and building societies offer joint accounts and this can be one of the easiest ways of arranging married finances. Having one account should mean there are no arguments about who pays which bills. Then again, it can lead to arguments about who spends most. The decision to set up a joint account should suit both partners and incomes. It is important to be honest from the outset about spending and outgoings, and remember that any debts are also jointly owned.

For some couples it is important to keep separate accounts and each take responsibility for different financial obligations. This might also avoid feelings of guilt if one of you is rather extravagant.

Another option is to set up a joint account to pay standing orders – like the mortgage and essential bills, where each partner pays a set amount into the account each month while still retaining their own separate accounts.

If you are in any doubt about the best way to organise your finances, make an appointment to see your bank or contact an independent financial adviser. At the same time you should think about setting up higher interest savings or deposit accounts.

Income tax

As far as your tax office is concerned, marriage makes no difference to your tax status and you are taxed individually.

If one of you is earning an income and the other is not, it is financially advantageous to keep any savings in the non-earning partner's name, as they will not be liable to pay tax on the interest.

Mortgages

A mortgage will probably be the largest loan a couple ever take out. If it is a joint mortgage, each partner is personally responsible for keeping up the payments and both risk being credit black-listed if repayments are not met. It is vital to get sound advice about the amount of money that should be borrowed, taking into account repayments and other expenses.

Mortgage rates vary and it is a good idea to shop around to find the best offer. Only borrow what you can afford to repay and remember the hidden costs involved in buying property: legal fees, solicitor's fees, search fees, survey, land registry, estate agent's fees (if you are also selling a property) and removals.

Both partners in a marriage have a claim to a share of any property, regardless of who owns it. When couples divorce, judges usually look at the needs of any children first, and often the property will remain with the children and the partner looking after them on a day-to-day basis.

Pensions

Pension schemes vary and marriage may make a difference to payments and returns. You should always check your individual policy to see what your spouse's entitlement would be. In some policies, wives receive only a proportion of the entitlement if their husband dies, and if they go on to remarry they may receive very little indeed. If you are not already involved in a pension scheme, it is sensible to take out a plan. Schemes on offer include employer's, government and private plans.

The law regarding pension sharing and divorce changed from 1 December 2000. The revised rules mean that the main wage-earner's retirement fund at the time of the divorce settlement is divided between each partner, allowing them both to invest in his or her own pension scheme. This change affects everyone, but women are more likely to be the beneficiaries. The Department of Social Security estimates the average value of a man's occupational pension to be £50,000 compared with an average of £7,000 for women. The change in the law to allow pension sharing should benefit around 50,000 women each year.

Life assurance

Life assurance is a safeguard. In return for a small monthly premium, your marriage partner will receive a lump sum in the event of your death. The amount paid usually covers the remainder owing on a mortgage, as well as helping with other outstanding debts. It is particularly important if there is only one wage-earner and especially if there are children.

Many employers offer life cover along with occupational pension funds. The life assurance policy taken out with your mortgage usually covers only the cost of the mortgage.

Do shop around for the best deal.

Age, sex and lifestyle all affect the premium you will have to pay, and it is important to choose the right policy for you.

Household insurance
BUILDINGS INSURANCE

If you have a mortgage, you must take out buildings insurance, which insures the fabric of the building.

Essentially this means the insurance company will pay for your property to be rebuilt if it is completely destroyed. Less dramatically, but equally importantly, it would also pay out for such eventualities as repairing a ceiling if it falls down through flood damage. Buildings insurance is based on the value of your property and is assessed by a surveyor for your mortgage company.

HOME CONTENTS INSURANCE

This covers your possessions, including furniture. An assessment of their value is made and premiums are based on the valuation, the security of your home and the type of cover you require. Most policies insure you against theft and damage, and some will also include accidental damage and provide cover when your possessions are away from your home.

HOME CONTENTS INSURANCE

✓ Do regularly update your contents insurance.
✓ Do inform your policy holder of any new items which should be specifically covered.
✓ Do shop around – policies and prices vary enormously.
✓ Do choose a reputable company or broker.
✓ Do remember to list valuable items separately.

WILLS

Marriage automatically invalidates any existing will you may have made. Drawing up a will ensures your assets and property are divided in the way you want after your death. Keeping a valid up-to-date will is particularly important if you own property and have children. It is wise to make specific provisions for your children's welfare in the event of both your deaths.

DRAWING UP A WILL

✓ Do consult a reputable solicitor (you don't want there to be any questions over the legality of your will).

✓ Do ask for an estimate of the cost.

Prenuptial agreements

In England and Wales, prenuptial agreements are not necessarily upheld by judges in divorce cases. They were originally an American idea and have gained notoriety through some well-publicised celebrity divorces, as well as very public, pre-matrimonial wrangling. Scottish courts tend to take such agreements much more seriously. Certainly, there is a far greater awareness of the existence of such contracts than there used to be.

Financial information

• **www.fsa.gov.uk** Financial Services Authority – regulatory body, useful if you want to know your rights or check out a financial institution.

• **www.find.co.uk** – directory for financial services and centre for independent financial advisers.

- **www.ft.com** *Financial Times* – up-to-date information, sound personal financial advice.

For personal finance try:
- **www.moneyextra.com**
- **www.emfinance.com**
- **www.moneynet.co.uk**

For mortgage advice:
- **www.charcolonline.co.uk** – independent adviser offering information on more than 400 mortgages from over 45 lenders.

For life insurance:
- **www.life-search.co.uk**

For insurance:
- **www.easycover.com**

For tax:
- **www.inlandrevenue.gov.uk**

MARRIED FINANCES

✔ Do discuss your finances together.

✔ Do organise professional advice.

✔ Do be honest about your own financial situation – including outgoings, debts and general spending.

✔ Do take out life assurance.

✔ Do join a pension scheme and make sure it provides for your spouse.

✓ Do think about setting up a savings account.
✓ Do pay bills on time.
✓ Do make a will.
✓ Don't forget to reassess your financial arrangements and policies regularly – there may be newer, better deals available.

WEDDING ANNIVERSARIES

Most couples choose to celebrate their wedding anniversary each year and so remember their wedding day. Each anniversary is traditionally associated with a different material.

1	Paper	13	Lace
2	Cotton or straw	14	Ivory
3	Leather	15	Crystal
4	Books or flowers	20	China
5	Wood	25	Silver
6	Iron	30	Pearl
7	Wool, copper or brass	35	Coral
8	Bronze	40	Ruby
9	Pottery	45	Sapphire
10	Tin	50	Golden
11	Steel	55	Emerald
12	Silk or linen	60	Diamond
		70	Platinum